NEVER THE SAME

C. Vincent O'Shaughnessy

NEVER THE SAME
Copyright © 1997 by C. Vincent O'Shaughnessy

ISBN No. 1-884920-11-X

Printed in the United States of America

Published by Jubilee Christian Center
175 Nortech Parkway
San Jose, California 95134

DEDICATION

My deepest appreciation to...

My wife Yvonne, my God-given helpmate,
    cherished friend, and precious gift. I thank
    God for our many happy years laboring
    together in the vineyard of the Lord,
    particularly at Paradise Christian Center
    and Christian Center School. Thank you,
    Yvonne, for the many hours of typing and
    helping with the editing of this book. I
    could not have done it without you.
To our daughters Kelly Ann and Seana Marie, and
    our foster-daughter, Jan-Kristine. Thank you
    for your prayers and encouragement.
To our dear friends who helped with the proofreading:
    Mary, Bev, John, and especially Tom who
    helped with the editing. To the faithful people
    of Paradise Christian Center.
A very special thanks to Pastors Dick and Carla Bernal
    and the Jubilee Christian Center Staff especially
    Virginia Obregon and Fellee Velasquez for
    publishing this book.
Above all, thanks be to God our Father for the gift of the
    Holy Spirit who guided us through this project.
    Deo Gratias.

CONTENTS

2

Foreword

It was early summer 1977, driving one evening to a business appointment, I was talking to Him - not really praying, just talking - about all the wonderful changes in my life since I'd surrendered all to Him only two months earlier. In the middle of it all, for no reason that I can explain, I blurted out a simple prayer: "Oh Lord, strengthen my faith!"

Vince O'Shaughnessy was the beginning of His answer to that prayer.

Before that week was out I learned of a home Bible study that had been going on for some months in our little town of Paradise, California. Though I'd grown up in a religious home and attended parochial schools for 12 years, the Bible was a brand new book to me and so I looked forward eagerly to the next meeting night.

The study had just begun as I arrived. For the next hour and a half I sat enthralled, straining to catch every soft-spoken word that flowed in honey-sweet brogue from a gentle Irish former priest who brought God and His Word to life in a way I'd never imagined much less experienced.

It wasn't theology. It was life. A living relationship with the Giver of Life.

That evening, living faith - not an organized set of beliefs, but a moment-to-moment adventure with God - began to take root in my heart.

In the years that followed, Vince and Yvonne O'Shaughnessy became spiritual parents to me and my wife, Nadine. It was from them we learned - not so much by what they taught as by what they modeled before us - the joy of knowing God's involvement in every smallest detail of our lives.

That's the essence of this precious little book. And I think it no accident, dear reader, that it has come at this moment into your hands.

Perhaps you've found religion empty and unsatis-fying. Don't feel guilty. Jesus found it empty too. What you desperately need, and what He came to bring you, is a living relationship with God who created you and whose plan for your life is the only way to genuine fulfillment.

Vince and Yvonne have been down that road. That's their story. And God has some wonderful things to show you in it.

Tom Manion
The Sower Ministries
Paradise, California

Introduction

A few years ago I was asked to write a brief testimony for publication in a book that contained the testimonies of 49 other former Roman Catholic priests who still had a ministry. It was the positive response to my testimony from people in various parts of the world that prompted the writing of this book.

I have tried to be transparent, open and honest in sharing my life experiences. Let me make it very clear that
I do not have the slightest bitterness towards my background as a Roman Catholic. On the contrary, I am very grateful for all the good things in my background and for having been raised in a Godly environment with real family values.

It is not my purpose to be controversial in writing this book. I felt that I needed to share the truths I had found in my study of God's Word, the Bible. Knowing and living by the truth of God's Word sets us free from the bondages of religious traditions of man.

Christianity is not a religion, but an ongoing, personal relationship with Jesus Christ.

As Yvonne and I began to grow spiritually, it was not a matter of leaving a particular denomination but of moving on in God beyond denominational limits while fellowshipping with like-minded believers that hungered and thirsted for more of God in our daily walk with Him.

Vince O'Shaughnessy

Turning Point

I walked out of the rectory one autumn day to meet Sister Yvonne Therese and her companion sister as they walked up the steps to our parish. Extending my hand in a hardy welcome, I invited the two nuns into my office.

"I hope you had no problem finding this place," I said.

"We got lost," laughed Sister Yvonne. "We tried to take a short cut through the mountains."

Giggling, they followed me down the hallway to my office.

I was the Roman Catholic Priest to a parish that covered most of western Siskiyou County at the northern tip of California.

I had requested assistance from the Sisters of the Holy Family to teach the children's catechism classes and was delighted when two sisters arrived to help me out in this remote but scenic part of California. My pastoral responsibilities covered three small communities that each had a church. Sometimes I thought of this area as a forgotten corner of the Lord's vineyard, and somewhat neglected spiritually and materially. During the year I had been there, I had thrown myself into building projects and ministering to keep from going crazy from loneliness.

In my office Sister Yvonne's effervescent

personality became apparent as she explained that although she had not yet made her final vows, she was in charge of this assignment. Consequently, she would be the one communicating with me. As this day stretched into weeks and months, Sister Yvonne and I began to enjoy our conversations together. We found that we shared compatible views on many subjects beyond the catechism classes.

This was a time of great unrest in America. President Kennedy had been assassinated. Young people who had grown disillusioned with the system had began questioning what life was all about. Although older I felt young at heart enough to identify with their concerns.

Sister Yvonne also felt drawn to these issues. One book we both read provided a new model for human communication—a model based on trust and transparency. The book, *On Becoming a Person*, had been written by psychologist Carl Rogers, and encouraged readers to examine their personalities and become more open in baring their souls. In following the example of the book, we inadvertently deepened our friendship as we identified with each other's soul searching. Nevertheless, our relationship remained on a professional level.

For my birthday that year Sister Yvonne gave me a gift that she had received after the tragic death of Martin Luther King. A piece of driftwood had been shaped into a mountain. A flag on top of the little mountain was inscribed with the words, "I have a dream."

When she gave it to me, I exclaimed, "You have a dream? I wonder if it is the same dream that I have?"

Immediately after I said this I felt embarrassed, because it sounded too intimate. Yvonne was taken aback by my reaction. Apparently, she had seen the gift as generic enough not to evoke my probing response.

One day a few weeks later we were in the midst of a discussion.

"How do you see me functioning in the ministry of the priesthood?" I asked Sister Yvonne. "Go ahead and be brutally honest with me."

"Father," she replied, "I see you doing all the right things, and I hear you saying all the right words from the pulpit. I see you fulfilling the role of a priest."

What does she mean? I wondered. *Is she saying that I'm going through the motions without feeling the ministry from my heart?*

Little did Sister Yvonne know that her words triggered an inner crisis about who I was and where I was headed in my ministry. I did not want to be seen as a phony priest who woodenly mediated between people and God, "holding to a form of godliness, but denying the power thereof" (2 Timothy 3:5). I began a period of intense prayer and soul-searching that culminated in a turning point.

On the last day of class before the Christmas break, I confronted Sister Yvonne before her catechism class. Even after repeated requests, she had still not given me her schedule for the new year.

"You need to give me the schedule for the new year before you leave today," I demanded.

Sister Yvonne looked flustered as she fumbled with her handbag and pulled out an envelope. Handing it to me, she said, "I shouldn't really do this, but I believe you need to know."

I unfolded the letter and examined it. It was her resignation from the sisterhood. The letter was informing her superior at the convent that she would respectfully finish out the year, so as not to inconvenience the order.

As I read this letter, it struck me that Sister

9

Yvonne would not be coming back to my parish, and I suddenly felt a great emptiness in my heart. I tried in vain to hold back the tears that flowed down my cheeks.

"Why are you crying?" asked Sister Yvonne.

"I don't know," I said. "I guess I'm in shock." Then I surprised myself by blurting out, "Don't you know that I love you?"

At that propitious moment, the children began to arrive for class and I left the room, leaving Sister Yvonne to face the students. That was the last time I saw Yvonne for several weeks.

The next day she departed from the convent at Mt. Shasta to return to her mother's home in the San Francisco Bay area.

That Christmas was a very lonely, dismal time for me, with deep snow cutting me off from the world. The truth of the saying, "absence makes the heart grow fonder," became very evident. I finally had to admit to myself and to God that I was in love with Yvonne. On Christmas Day I telephoned her.

"I want to wish you a Merry Christmas, and tell you that I miss you," I said.

"Thank you," she responded.

"I also want to tell you that I am seriously considering leaving the priesthood."

"You can't do that, and you can't love me," she protested. "You are a priest. I can't stand the thought of being the reason you leave the priesthood. Let's just be friends."

The phrase, "Let's just be friends," kept coming back to me. From the moment that we met, I had felt an instant rapport with Yvonne—as though we were long-lost friends. For many years I had been counseling couples preparing for marriage to be sure that first of all they were friends. That seemed an essential foundation for a successful relationship.

I got some solace from the fact that Yvonne considered me a friend. But her words, "You are a priest, you can't love me," were like a dagger in my heart.

But she was right. I was a Catholic priest. I can't fall in love with a nun. How did I get myself into this mess?

Memories

Born in West Limerick, Ireland, the youngest of three girls and four boys, I was raised on a farm in the horse and buggy days of the late 1920s. I fondly remember getting rides aplenty.

Our family did the regular chores of milking the cows by hand, tilling the soil, "saving the hay," planting and reaping various crops, and feeding the chickens, pigs, horses, donkeys and ducks. Milking the cows every morning and evening, I grew quite attached to some of them. Each one had a name. Old Nellie was one of my favorites, and when she died, my dad dug a grave for her.

After she was buried, I asked him, "Is Nellie in heaven?"

"No, there is no heaven for animals," he replied.

"You mean Nellie will never see another cow?" I cried. I felt very upset by this, trying to visualize a state of nothingness for Nellie. I began to question this theology, wondering, *what if there is no heaven for me?*

During the World War II years fuel came to be in short supply. My brothers and I would dig peat from the bog for fire fuel. After breakfast at dawn, we headed out on the horse cart for the fifteen mile journey to the bog. The peat was dug out layer by layer to a depth of about six feet, then placed to dry on the bank. It was back-breaking work! By noon we were starving, so we made a turf fire for tea. We also boiled a pot of potatoes in the turf fire, and ate the ham sandwiches my mother had sent. In the late afternoon we devoured her apple pie. After ten hours of digging, we headed home and fell into bed exhausted.

I rolled out of bed each morning onto my knees to say the morning prayers my mother had taught me. I'd begin with the Morning Offering: "Oh, Jesus, through the most pure heart of Mary, I give you this day...." Then I'd move on to the Lord's Prayer and the Hail Mary prayer.

From my earliest childhood, I assumed that I had to go through Mary to reach Jesus. Each evening I knelt with my family in the kitchen-living room to pray the rosary. The rosary consists of five repetitions of one Our Father, followed by ten Hail Mary's. The add-ons to the rosary seemed to go on forever. We'd pray three Hail Mary's for each neighbor who had a problem, and the same for every deceased relative or friend. By the time we'd finish the long list my knees would be killing me. Yet there remained the Litany of Saints which seemed endless, as we responded to each saint's name with, "Pray for us." At the tender age of four, I thought we were saying "papers," an indication of my lack of understanding of these rituals!

My father prayed often to St. Joseph for help in making him a good husband and father. He was a kind and gentle man, a man in whom there was no guile. I loved him very much.

Every morning my dad would deliver the cows' milk to the creamery, and when he came back with the newspaper, my mother's first words would be, "Who's dead today?"

Everybody read the obituaries first because funerals were one of the big social events of the community. Funerals meant an all-night wake, with neighbors visiting the next day bringing food. The coffin would rest in church overnight before mass.

I used to have to pass by the family graveyard on my way home. Often this was in the dark. I got really scared, especially after hearing ghost stories at the neighbor's house. Even the hedges seemed like phantoms following me. One evening I saw a black apparition in front of me. Running in panic down the long driveway, I turned and discovered that it was our old black mare.

My mother was something else. About five-feet-two, her eyes of blue flashed in fun or anger according to the carryings-on around her. Although my name is Charles Vincent, she insisted I be called Vincent, as the possibility of being called 'Charlie' was too undignified. I resented this snobbery and the way she ruled the roost, but I admired the efficient way in which she got things done.

My mother would not let me play with the neighbor's children because they were beneath us socially.

There is one spanking I will never forget. One fine summer evening I went into the apple orchard, filled my pockets with apples, and headed out to a farm laborer's house to play with the boys and share my apples. But my mother found me out, and administered a real spanking. The spanking hurt plenty, but I held on to my determination not to judge people according to social or economic class.

As was the custom in those days, I started school at age four. The first year we were known as the "Do a cloughs," Gaelic for 2:00 p.m., the time our school day ended. The second year we were called the "Low Infant Class" and the third year the "High Infant Class."

The infant school and primary school (elementary) system in Ireland, which is called the National School

System was managed by the local Roman Catholic Parish priest. This man hired and fired staff, exercising a good deal of power in the school community.

During my six years in elementary school, the first class each morning was catechism, a special class for Roman Catholic indoctrination. There was a series of questions and answers which we had to memorize. If you missed the answer to a single question, you got two swats of a stick, one on each hand, sometimes hard enough to cause welts. Some of the teachers were sadistic in administering punishment rather than utilizing wise discipline. I'm sure this left scars on many a young psyche, and marred their understanding of God's love for children.

Our family never missed Mass on Sunday unless we were seriously ill. We were taught that you could go to hell for committing this deadly sin, if you died before confessing to a priest and receiving forgiveness. The priests were held in awe that bordered on idolatry. While some priests were stern and harsh, others were fun-loving and inspiring to be around.

A fiery young priest whom I greatly admired gave my sisters and me rides in his automobile, a rare commodity in those days, especially in the rural areas. Father Michael liked our family and visited frequently in our home. My parents wined and dined him, and gave him the royal treatment.

When I was about ten, a freak accident drew focus to my growing desire to someday become a priest. I was helping my brother John clean off the hay cutting bar when suddenly he moved the cog wheel. This caused the blades to engage and cut an inch off my right index finger.

My first reaction was not to be afraid of the blood, but to cry out in horror, "Now I can't be a priest! I can't become a priest!"

I'd heard that a boy could not become a priest if his thumbs and index fingers were mutilated, because they needed to be perfect for handling the host during Mass.

Completing elementary school, I passed the national exam necessary to advance to high school. I rode my bicycle ten miles round trip each day, rain or shine, and labored at several hours of homework each evening.

After two years of high school, I planned to join my brother Michael the following fall at a Jesuit boarding high school, Mungret College. The need to serve God was growing stronger inside me. My mother's constant prayers and the years of hearing Father Michael's dynamic sermons had deeply influenced me. Now all I cared about was becoming a priest.

During summer vacation, however, I met a priest from another religious order. I shared with him that I felt a call to serve God. He spent a lot of time with me, encouraging me to attend the boarding school operated by his particular order. I decided to follow his urging, and enrolled for the fall in his order's school instead of Mungret College.

Pathway to Priesthood

I have few happy memories of my time in boarding school. There were plenty of rules, strictly enforced, with dire consequences for violations. There was no hot water in the bathrooms, so our showers, especially in the winter, were freezing cold.

Most of my teachers were kind and fair. There were occasions when I felt their spiritual depth. One prayer I was taught especially sticks in my mind: "Here I am, Lord. I surrender. I want to serve You. I love You above all things. Do with me what You will."

But one teacher was cruel and sadistic. He found pleasure in pulling my hair and twisting my arm until I cried out in pain. I figured that I had to endure this kind of abuse if I were ever to succeed in becoming one of those revered priests. This man had a violent temper and when in a rage would literally shake like a leaf in the wind. I still have nightmares about my encounters with him.

I finished my senior year and together with several classmates advanced to the novitiate, a kind of spiritual boot camp almost like a prison where individual identity is systematically eradicated. The novice master was a sergeant-major type determined to break our spirit. With ever-increasing pressure he sought to mold us into the image of what he thought we should be.

On certain days we were supposed to wear rough-edged chains around our bare waist and on our arms or thighs. One evening each week we gathered in a dark corridor and during the recitation of Psalm 51, known as the Miserere, ("Have mercy on me, O Lord...") we dropped our pants and underpants and flogged our derrieres with a kind of cat-o-nine tails. There were other forms of mortification and humiliation which I resisted because they seemed threatening to my identity as a person.

One day after about six months in the novitiate, completely without warning, the novice master presented me and some of my classmates with a train ticket to our respective homes. We had been summarily dismissed without any explanation whatsoever. I felt like a complete failure. On that lonely train ride home, as the plaintive whistle blew, I kept thinking, *Now what am I going to do?*

Upon returning home, I still felt a strong call of God on my life. In the Ireland of those days, the only way one could serve God was as a priest, brother or nun. There was no place for lay ministry, other than as an altar boy. I entered a missionary college seminary to study for the priesthood. The rigorous program consisted of two years of philosophy and four years of theology, together with canon law and some other subjects. We were required to memorize many "Si quis dixerits", each ending with "Anathema sit." This meant that whoever dared to disagree with Roman Catholic doctrine would be cursed, banished, and excommunicated.

My seminary days were the best of times and the worst of times. Insecurity was the order of the day. Each day we wondered who would be expelled next. One president of the college, nicknamed "the Beagle", told us in chapel that he would not hesitate to drop any one of us like a hot potato at any time. It was a matter of survival of the fittest and I was determined to survive. I buckled down, studied hard, and gained a good reputation with most of the faculty.

All of us in the seminary had nicknames. Mine was "the Pope." My two best friends were called "Cardinal Tarrantini" and Cardinal Meskillini." The faculty members also had nicknames. There were three presidents during my time. The first one we called "little Johnny" because he was so short. The next was "the Beagle" because he was always sniffing around. The third one was "Chaucer" because of his fondness for old English writings.

One faculty member nicknamed "Ducky," whom I greatly admired, later became an archbishop and tells the story of being asked the difference between a bishop and archbishop. He placed his hands on his broad girth and replied, "Mainly the arch!"

After about two years, when it became apparent I would meet the academic standards, seemingly the only criteria by which a student was judged, the seminary president called me to his office. He asked me where I would like to serve as a diocesan priest, working under the bishop of a diocese—a geographical area administered and supervised by a bishop or archbishop.

"It makes no difference to me," I said, "as long as I go where there is a real need."

My reply seemed to shock him since most students were very picky about where they wanted to go. Not many were volunteering for far away places like Australia and New Zealand. He informed me that he was expecting a visit from the Bishop of Ballarat, Australia, and that he would arrange an interview if I desired. The result of the interview was that I conditionally agreed to go to Australia following my ordination in four years time.

A few months later a very dynamic young bishop from New Zealand spoke to the student body. After an impassioned appeal for help for his diocese, he invited the students to talk with him privately. I was drawn to respond to his appeal and explained to him my conditional agreement with the bishop of Ballarat. The outcome of our discussion was that the New Zealand bishop arranged for a release so that I could go to his diocese where the need was greater.

Several months later the college president, a golfing friend of my Uncle Michael, called me to his office.

"I've been thinking," he said, "how easy you made it for me to send you anywhere in the world. I have a letter here from the bishop of Sacramento, California, requesting a student who would be ordained three years hence. I would like you to accept this request."

"But what about our agreement with the bishop of New Zealand?" I asked.

"I have already taken care of that," he responded. "You are free to accept the Sacramento invitation, and I'd like you to do so." That settled the matter. Three years later at the age of twenty-six, I would be headed for beautiful northern California. However, I still had three more years in the seminary.

When I refer to the seminary today, I call it the "cemetery." I might as well have spent six years digging graves for all that I learned of any practical value for the work of the ministry. In retrospect, I see all the non-practical training we received as irrelevant to ministers of the Gospel. I learned more in my first year on the job than during six years of seminary.

It grieves me to think that in all those years the Bible, the Word of God, was just filling a space on my bookshelf as hour after hour I poured through man-made laws and teachings. We did no real study of the Bible, only an academic smattering—nothing of any depth or consequence. I often regret that no one ever encouraged me to study the Scriptures during those six long years. But I realize that since I was not born again, it probably would not have been meaningful to me. The eyes of my understanding would not have been open to Divine revelation.

Those six long years in the seminary were mostly an exercise in self preservation; trying to stay one step ahead of "the gods," as we referred to the faculty.

In my fourth year a group of young men came to the seminary as students. This group had a strong leader, a very good athlete. He had a reputation as a sprinter, which also happened to be my area of skill. When the annual sports day came around, we ended up competing in the finals of the sixty, one-hundred and the two-twenty yard dashes. I beat him in two of the three events. This resulted in a lot of antagonism toward me by him and his followers. The camp was now divided: he and his friends versus me and mine. It was decided that the only way to resolve the matter was a showdown between the two of us.

A time and a place was set for this bare-fisted duel. The only witnesses were to be two friends from each side. The fatal day arrived. I say fatal because had it been discovered by the powers that be, it would have meant automatic expulsion. Fortunately, his side decided not to risk the showdown. A short time later he left the seminary.

I felt lucky to have stayed out of trouble for the rest of my stay, since two-thirds of my original classmates never made it to the end. The long-awaited day of ordination finally came, a memorable occasion with a big reception for family and friends. The celebration continued through the next day, the day of my first mass, when most of the people of the parish showed up for the young priest's first blessing.

I have many pictures recalling that momentous

occasion, undoubtedly the most significant and happiest event up to that point in my life. Apart from having succeeded in surviving a very grueling six-year course, I also felt a deep spiritual significance in my ordination. I was now delegated by God to be "a priest forever according to the order of Melchizedek" (Psalm 110:4; Hebrews. 5:6). I believed that God had conferred on me the greatest privilege and honor available to man, that of being an alter Christus—another Christ. I was now the Lord's representative on earth.

I shed tears of joy, and felt humility and gratitude to God and to all who helped me along the way. I believed that I now had the spiritual power and authority to forgive sin on His behalf in the confessional, and to change bread and wine into His body and blood in the sacrifice of the Mass. I had memorized the formulas: "Ego te absolvo" (I absolve you); "Hoc est corpus meum" (this is My body); and "Hic est calix sanguinis mei" (this is the cup of My blood).

I had poured out my heart to God since boyhood to see the reality of this day. God had answered my prayer. I sincerely wanted to know Him, love Him, and serve Him. I was willing to leave father, mother, brothers, sisters and homeland to go to the uttermost parts of the earth.

From a human point of view, I felt delighted to have brought happiness to my family, relatives and friends as they rejoiced with me. It was considered a status symbol to have a priest in the family. Now we had two, as my brother Michael had been ordained in San Antonio, Texas, three years earlier.

It was the dream of every Irish parent to have a priest in the family—a mediator between man and God. Now my parents' dream had come true!

California, Here I Come

After a brief vacation at home, I set sail for New York along with several other recently ordained priests. Leaving home and family was not easy. Apart from trips to Lourdes in France, and Rome, I had never ventured far from home.

My parents were getting up in years and I did not know if I would ever see them again. These were the days when crossing the Atlantic Ocean to America meant getting on a ship rather than on an airplane. I set sail from Cobh Harbor, as many Irish had done during the past century, beginning with the potato famine in the 1840s. Unlike the coffin ships of yore, mine was a luxury liner of the famed British Cunard line. It took six days to cross the Atlantic to New York where I was met by friends of our family. For the next two weeks they took me all over the area to see the sights and places of interest.

One day in downtown Manhattan, we came to an intersection where a police officer was directing traffic. My friend called out to him, "Hey, Mike Shaughnessy! Do you want to meet a namesake from the auld sod?" I couldn't believe what happened next. Mike left the traffic at a standstill and came over to our car to greet me and welcome me to America.

The other thing I remember about New York was the horrible heat and especially the humidity, having been used to the cool climate of Ireland.

After two weeks in New York, I boarded a train to cross the United States to California, a trip which took three days. It was an interesting and informative trip. We were met by an uncle of one of my fellow priests at a little train station at a town called Crockett. For the next two weeks he took us all over the San Francisco Bay Area and the Napa Valley wine country.

Following these two weeks, we were delivered to the Chancery office of the Diocese of Sacramento to receive our assignments. My first assignment was nearby at the Cathedral in downtown Sacramento, one block from the State Capitol.

The culture shock was terrific for a farm gossun (boy) who had been used to roaming the green fields around his home in Ireland. Even so, I began my priestly duties with zeal and commitment to the work of the ministry. I was determined to do the best job and be the very best priest that I could be.

My room was on the third floor of the Cathedral rectory. The room had just been vacated by a man who had a problem common among Catholic priests. It took me several trips to the dumpster to get rid of all the empty bottles I found in drawers and closets.

I felt grieved, because at this time I was a teetotaler and belonged to an Irish organization called the Pioneer Total Abstinence Association (PTAA). We identified ourselves by wearing a red heart-shaped pin. When Irish people saw a person wearing such an emblem, they would not offer alcoholic drinks. Otherwise you were expected to belly-up to the bar and drink with the best of them.

At the Cathedral I spent long hours in the confessional booth, not wanting to walk out while people were still waiting in line. But I noticed that walking out of the confessional as soon as the time was up did not seem to bother the other priests. The result was that on Saturdays I used to show up late for dinner and was made fun of by the others for my service to the late-comers, especially the Mexican-Americans. God gave me a special love for these humble, unassuming people, who in turn loved their padrecito and would kneel and kiss my hand. This experience touched and humbled me. I even delayed the celebration of my birthday by one day in order to celebrate with them their great annual feast of Our Lady of Guadalupe on December 12.

My first senior pastor was an austere, self-disciplined man who kept to himself except for mealtimes. After six months at the Cathedral, the senior pastor asked me if I would be interested in a vacancy at a large parish in the suburbs, which had an all-native Irish staff. I accepted the offer.

At first it looked as though I had gone from the frying pan into the fire. My new senior pastor, the Monsignor, was a semi-invalid with three associate pastors. I soon found out that the power behind the throne was the housekeeper, the Monsignor's sister. She answered all the doorbells and phone calls and routed them to her brother, whether people asked for him or not.

The kitchen was out-of-bounds and so was the dining room, unless invited by the housekeeper to come in for meals. In the mornings, we waited in the living room for her invitation to breakfast. "Gyne (go in) to your mush, boys," she would brusquely quip. One day she chased one of the associate priests out of the kitchen with a carving knife. He grabbed a chair to keep from being stabbed.

I remained in that parish for six years. The old pastor's health grew progressively worse. Believe it or not, the housekeeper took a liking to me. We got along well for the duration of my time, and I took on more and more responsibility in running the parish.

In fact, I got caught up in work-a-holism, a general busyness that never seemed to quit. This caused my spiritual life to suffer. I still spent some time in prayer before and after Mass, and daily read the breviary, the official prayer of the clergy, but I had little or no emotional contact with God. I did things by rote, and worked for efficiency, not inspiration.

Each Saturday evening I would prepare my sermon from the outline supplied by the Diocese. I enjoyed preaching as I had learned how to appeal to the emotions. I made the people feel good and on that score I was considered a good preacher. Yet looking back I realize that I had no idea how to minister to the people in the power of the Holy Spirit.

And God was trying to tell me so.

One morning when I was about five years into the priesthood, I was standing in front of the church waiting for a funeral to arrive, wearing the vestments for the funeral mass. There was no one around except a little black boy who looked to be about five or six years old. He walked up to me and around me, sizing me up with his big brown eyes.

Finally, he spoke, saying, "Who are you? You a preacher?" Then he looked me right in the eye and said, "Are you saved?"

I don't remember my response. I probably didn't respond at all. Only twelve years later did I realize that this little boy was asking me the most important question of my life. Sadly, I had no idea what he was talking about. Obviously, the boy understood what it meant to be saved. Picture the scene: God was trying to reach me through this little boy, yet I paid no attention to what he was saying.

Eventually I was transferred to northern California, near the Oregon border. That's where I met Sister Yvonne Therese.

The Agony

In the weeks and months that followed my encounter with Sister Yvonne, I cried out to God for direction in my life. Should I leave the priesthood or should I try to hang in there? Could I change my "going-through-the-motions" style of ministry of which Yvonne had made me aware? I decided to give it a try. Calling the best mission-giver I knew, I invited him to come and hold a mission (revival) in an effort to bring spiritual renewal to my life and to the parish.

The mission was held the first week of Lent, but I found myself deeply disappointed. The man was loud and bombastic, and his message rang hollow and devoid of a heart for God. He, too, had a "form of godliness, but none of the power thereof" (2 Tim. 3:5). Paul had warned Timothy to "avoid such men as these."

With great pain in my heart, I decided to leave the priesthood. Even though I had tried to be a good priest by observing all the rules, I now knew this wasn't enough to sustain my remaining a priest.

I wrote to Yvonne to tell her of my final, irrevocable decision and asked if I could come and talk with her over dinner. She agreed and we had a long dinner session at the Concord Inn next to her home town of Pleasant Hill.

"I've decided to leave the priesthood no matter what happens with you and me," I told her.

But she still kept insisting, "No, Vince, you can't

leave. You just can't do that."

"Why not?" I asked. "You left the convent of your own free will. Why don't I have the same choice? What if you had come to me to share your decision as I'm sharing with you, and I responded, "No, Yvonne, you can't do that. You can't leave the convent."

Suddenly she realized what she was doing to me. "I am so sorry, Vince," she whispered with eyes tearing. "I was wrong in trying to tell you what you can or cannot do. But if you do leave, you have to know it's God's will for you, just as I knew that it was God's will for me."

I reassured Yvonne that I had prayed long and hard about my decision and was sure that it was God's will for me. With that reassurance, we agreed to place our friendship in the hands of God for His will to be fulfilled.

I wrote to my bishop requesting that he seek a dispensation for me from Rome. I told him I had secured an interim priest to cover the parish for two months following my departure.

On Easter Sunday, I celebrated Mass for the last time and shared my decision with the congregation. It was one of the hardest things I have ever done. These precious people truly loved their priest and were broken-hearted. We hugged and cried together.

The next day I set out for the San Francisco Bay Area with my few belongings packed in a little trailer behind the parish car. I stopped in Sacramento to visit briefly with the bishop, and to assure him that I would make arrangements to get the parish car back to the Diocese.

He asked me for the pink slip, wrote on it, and handed it back to me saying, "Vince, enjoy it. Now it is yours. You will need wheels." I will always remember his gracious gesture of kindness.

Is God helping me leave the priesthood? I wondered as I pulled out of Sacramento.

I arrived in Oakland where Yvonne had her apartment. After leaving the convent, she had secured a good job with a prominent law firm in Alameda. Now she moved back to her mother's house in Pleasant Hill so I could occupy her apartment. It was a very peaceful place, a kind of penthouse overlooking Lake Merritt.

Here I began a healing process from the awful trauma that followed my decision to leave the priesthood. Dispirited thoughts coursed through me: *I'm nobody. I've failed. What am I, if not a priest?* Shame weighed heavy on me, along with fear about how my family in Ireland would respond. This process extended over a couple of months, during which time I saw Yvonne each evening when she came to prepare dinner, before returning to her mother's home. After many a conversation I felt lighter, as though someone truly accepted and understood me. *Is God here with us in our talks?* I sometimes asked myself.

We began to talk about the prospect of marriage and counseled with some highly respected friends, including some of my priest friends. I had decided that I would not officially ask Yvonne to marry me until I had secured a job. During this time I spent my days praying and filling out employment applications.

One day a friend at the Alameda Probation Department, a former priest, gave me an application that had come across his desk from Colusa County Probation Department. I filled it out and mailed it, went for an interview, and got the job—praise the Lord!

My new job necessitated my moving to Colusa, over one hundred miles from Oakland and from Yvonne. Again, absence made our hearts grow fonder and our phone lines were kept busy in the evenings. Yvonne moved back to her apartment.

One weekend Yvonne and I went for dinner at the Moonraker in Pacifica, on the coast near San Francisco. There, as the moon sent shafts of silver light from heaven across the ocean waves, I formally popped the question. I felt like shouting when Yvonne responded as I had hoped she would.

A few weeks later we were married. In all my excitement I forgot that we needed at least one wedding ring. We had to borrow a ring from Yvonne's maid of honor, Gretchen. Later Yvonne gave me a beautiful Celtic wedding ring with an inscription that read, "I have a dream!"

A close friend of mine in the inner circle of the Diocese advised me that the fastest way to get my dispensation would be to forward our marriage certificate to the bishop. We did this and the dispensation process got a jump start. Even so, we were hoping to keep our marriage a secret until the dispensation was granted.

The law firm which employed Yvonne liked her work so well that they offered her several incentives to stay, including a considerable raise in salary. Yvonne agreed to stay a couple of months so that her replacement could be trained.

We were only married a week or so when one afternoon, upon returning to my office in Colusa, I found a note from my secretary that read, "Vince, call Mrs. O'Shaughnessy."

"Who's this Mrs. O'Shaughnessy?" I asked. "My mother is in heaven."

"Come on, Vince," she chuckled. "We know that you and Yvonne are married. My mother read it in the vital statistics the other day."

Immediately I called Yvonne. "Honey, are you sitting down? I have a slight shock for you. Our great

34

secret is no secret anymore."

"Oh, my goodness," she gasped, "What if my mother finds out from someone else? I had better tell her myself."

We both knew that Yvonne's mother would be adamantly opposed to our marriage. She had made it clear on each of my visits to her home that she did not approve of me as a suitor for her daughter.

It was customary for Yvonne to take her mother grocery shopping on Saturdays. In fear and trepidation, she picked up her mother as usual, but could not get up the courage to tell her the news.

When they returned with the groceries, Yvonne took them into the house. Standing in the doorway, she blurted out, "By the way, Mom, I have something to tell you. Vince and I are married."

With that, she left her mother standing there with her mouth open, and drove to her apartment where I was visiting for the weekend.

She literally fell into my arms with exhaustion saying, "I did it, I did it. I told my mother we are married. I doubt if she will ever speak to me again."

For the next month her mother gave Yvonne the stone-cold silent treatment on their Saturday grocery trips. We prayed and committed this unpleasant situation to the Lord.

Yvonne was preparing to move to Colusa. The last day at the law firm she got a terrible pain in her lower back and had to leave the office as the pain intensified. Not knowing where else to turn, she headed for her mother's home, where she literally collapsed on the couch. Her mother called several doctors' offices trying to get an appointment, but to no avail. Yvonne and her mother drove directly to the hospital emergency unit for treatment.

The doctor told Yvonne that she could not travel. Since her apartment was twenty miles away, she had no place to go except to her mother's home. This medical emergency required her mother to notify me. Needless to say, I wasted no time in covering the hundred and twenty miles, all the while crying out to God on behalf of my wife. Yvonne's diagnosis was a severe kidney infection. But there was some good news, too. The medical examination revealed that my precious wife was pregnant. Hallelujah!

With Yvonne confined to bed for a few days, my mother-in-law and I simply had to talk to each other. She slowly discovered that she liked me and could accept me into the family. In the process, the fractured relationship between Yvonne and her mom was also healed. When Yvonne was well enough to travel, we headed out for Colusa, where I had rented a cute, little two-bedroom house.

God had answered our prayers and worked everything out in His own unique way!

The Ecstasy

It was a great day when our dispensation came and our marriage was blessed by the Catholic Church. This was very important to us, as we were still committed Catholics, and intended to remain so. Many of Yvonne's family, including her mom, came for the blessing ceremony. The eighty-year-old monsignor entered the church all dressed up in his red robes. I had known and liked this man for many years.

Monsignor's first comment was precious.

"Vince," he said, "it's been a long time since I have had an occasion that justified dressing up like this, but today I want to honor you and Yvonne. If I were fifty years younger, I would probably choose the same path that you have chosen. Congratulations."

His comment confirmed my belief that many of my former peers wished they had the courage to do what I had done. Indeed, some priests who were wrestling with issues of celibacy and marriage sought us out for counseling over the years. A few were able to make the break, but most could not bring themselves to the final decision.

The local pastor and his associate became our friends, and we praised God for their sensitivity to our needs. Visiting our humble abode, they realized that we lacked most household items. In fact, all we had was a studio couch, a lazy-boy chair, and a few kitchen items. The associate pastor made a list of our basic needs and within a few days had supplied us with what we needed. One of his resources was the parish convent, which had been vacated by the sisters, as the parish school was discontinued for lack of teaching nuns. The local pastor gave Yvonne the job of director of the parish Confraternity of Christian Doctrine program which helped us financially.

The next highlight in our life was the birth of Kelly Ann, our precious daughter. We felt ecstatic when Kelly was born. In those days, the father was not allowed into the delivery room, but the local doctor had become a friend. He allowed me to witness the birth. During Yvonne's labor, I was surrounded by a half-dozen student nurses. Together we rooted for Yvonne at each contraction. In fact, I identified so closely with Yvonne's labor that the next day my stomach muscles ached.

For exercise we'd ride our bikes in the evenings, carrying the baby in a pouch. We enjoyed looking at houses that were for sale, just for the fun of it, as one window shops when one has no money to buy. One evening we stopped to look at a very nice house. The next morning I was prosecuting a case in the Juvenile Court when the defense attorney approached me during a recess in the proceedings.

"I saw you and your wife looking at the house next door to mine last night," he said. "Are you interested in buying it?"

"We couldn't even afford the fancy knob on the front door," I laughed. "We just like to look."

"I'll loan you the down payment and you can pay it back as you are able. We would be delighted to have you as our neighbors."

I could scarcely believe what I was hearing, as he and I were just professional acquaintances. However, he insisted and we took him up on the offer.

Soon we were settled into our new home and we gave God all the glory. We were mindful of Ephesians 3:20-21, "Now to Him who is able to do exceeding abundantly beyond all that we ask or think, according to the power that works within us, to Him be glory in the church and in Christ Jesus to all the generations forever and ever."

On Kelly's first birthday we planted a Kelly green tree in the front yard as a reminder of God's great blessings in this place. The tree is now a full-grown evergreen. We still drive by once in a while to remind ourselves of God's goodness.

We settled into our new home feeling very thankful that God had made a way for us to marry and have good jobs, a new home, and a delightful daughter. We had obtained the "American dream" with its worldly components, yet something was missing in our lives. I couldn't put my finger on it, but sensed that it was spiritual. We were living like "good" Catholics, attending church faithfully and doing all the things that good Catholics are supposed to do. Yet each Sunday morning as we returned home from Mass, we felt unfulfilled and spiritually dry.

We talked our feelings over, but did not know why we felt this way or how to change it. Most of our friends at that time were priests who did not have the answer when we tried to discuss it with them. Gradually, we came to an awareness that we had a spiritual hunger that was not being fulfilled. We began to pray to God for help.

Here we were with all the trappings of religion, but had to acknowledge a void in our hearts. *What needs to happen for God to fill this void?* we wondered.

Born Again

One evening we were invited to a neighboring parish. After dinner we disclosed our hunger for more of God.

The pastor got up to get a little book from his bookshelf saying, "Maybe this would be helpful."

The book was called *Catholic Pentecostals*, and had been written by Kevin Ranaghan, a professor at Notre Dame University in South Bend, Indiana. When we got home Yvonne read it immediately, literally devouring it. She was very excited about the testimonies of Catholics who had discovered a spiritual rebirth and the infilling of the Holy Spirit. This terminology was foreign to us as Catholics, but Yvonne discerned that we were experiencing the same hunger these people had known prior to their being born again and baptized in the Holy Spirit.

My first reaction to the title of *Catholic Pentecostals* was negative. To me the terms "Catholic" and "Pentecostal" were like oil and water, diametrically opposed to each other. I didn't bother to read the book. But everywhere I went in the house, the little book seemed to follow me.

One day, looking for something to read, I picked it up. It drew me in. I had to admit what these Catholics were describing in their testimonies was exactly what I was seeking—a personal relationship with Jesus, and a manifestation of His power in my life. Without this, I knew that I could not live the Christian life that Jesus was calling me to live. Like many others, I had learned to talk the talk, but lacked the joy and power to walk the walk.

Soon after this, a man with whom we were not acquainted but who had heard about us, came to our door with a packet.

"God told me to bring you this," he said, holding it out to me. Then he turned and left. The packet contained two audio tapes by the Ranaghans, explaining in more detail about being born again and baptized in the Holy Spirit. The package also contained a book called *Nine O'Clock in the Morning*, by Father Dennis Bennett. This book is his testimony of how as pastor of a large church in Los Angeles, he was born again and baptized in the Holy Spirit. As a result of sharing his joy, he was removed from his parish and sent to pastor a little dying parish in an impoverished area of Seattle, Washington.

Soon the Seattle parish exploded with new life in Christ and the blessings of the Holy Spirit. Many hundreds of people came to experience Jesus and the Holy Spirit. This little church became a great Christian center from which the fire of the Holy Spirit began to spread across America. This wave of Holy Spirit glory affected nearly every denomination, and contributed to the Catholic charismatic renewal.

This renewal, which began at Notre Dame University, spread to other Catholic universities, as young people hungered for more of God. Both Ranaghan's and Father Bennett's books were very helpful to me.

Soon after we read these books, Yvonne and I were invited to a meeting where a Catholic nun and a Catholic medical doctor were to share their testimonies of how they were born again and filled with the Holy Spirit.

The Catholic nun's testimony ministered powerfully to Yvonne, as she had experienced some similar things in the convent. God used the doctor's testimony to speak to me, as I could relate to what he was sharing. As a Catholic, he had thought he was a Christian, and for that matter, so had I. Then he asked a bomb-shell question: "If you were to die tonight, are you sure of going to heaven? Are you sure of your salvation?"

I found myself thinking, *I don't know*, and then, *I hope so*. I recalled the Roman Catholic teaching that one has to go through purgatory to be cleansed of sin before entering into God's presence.

The doctor explained that Jesus paid in full for all sin with His shed blood on the cross of Calvary. All who accept Him as Savior will be saved, but those who reject Him, or look to their own works to save them, will be lost. He read Romans 10:9-10: "If you confess with your mouth Jesus is Lord, and believe in your heart that God raised Him from the dead, you shall be saved; for with the heart man believes, resulting in righteousness, and with the mouth he confesses, resulting in salvation."

This scripture was telling me that both heart and mouth are involved in the process of salvation. First, I had to believe in my heart that God's Word was true. Then I needed to confess my faith in God's plan of salvation through the blood of Christ that was shed for me. I had to speak this truth, publicly acknowledging Christ as my Savior. I understood that this process is wholly a matter of faith, not feeling.

I learned that I didn't have to wait until I died to receive my inheritance. "Giving thanks to the Father, who has qualified and made us fit to share the portion which is the inheritance of the saints in the Light" (Colossians 1:12). As a child of God I could receive all that belonged to me through the riches of Christ right now. "Do not be afraid, little flock, for your Father has chosen gladly to give you the kingdom" (Luke 12:32).

When the altar call, or invitation to make Jesus Lord of our life was given, guess who were the first ones up there? Right—Vince and Yvonne. We immediately began to experience new life in Christ. Our prayer life became more fulfilling and the Bible, the Word of God, began to come alive as we prayerfully meditated on what our Father was saying to us as His children.

I finally understood the question that little black boy had asked me twelve years earlier. I had to honestly admit that until now, I had not made Jesus the Lord of my life. I was forty-five years old before I understood what it meant to be saved, to be born again.

Baptism in the Holy Spirit

I cannot explain why there was no prayer for the baptism in the Holy Spirit the night we were born again, except to say that God knows what is best. He knew we were not ready. We had not yet received any teaching on the infilling or baptism in the Holy Spirit. But now we were very interested in receiving all that God had for us.

We attended a Full Gospel Businessmen's meeting shortly after we were saved. We went with a certain measure of fear and trepidation, as we had heard some stories of weird things happening like people falling down or being "slain in the Spirit," a term completely foreign to us. We were greeted at the door by the president of the chapter, a man from Beale Air Force Base named Cleve Howard. It was the first time I had ever been hugged by a black man, and I will always remember the love of God that flowed to me through this man. It felt as though I was being hugged by Jesus Himself.

The meeting began with praise and worship, led by a young airman. This was our first experience of seeing people worship in the Spirit since we had only recently been saved. As these people were worshipping God with their eyes closed and their hands raised, we were observing the glory of God radiating from their faces. This was the kind of worship we had longed for. When the speaker finished sharing his testimony, he began to minister and people began to fall down. If we had been close to an exit, we probably would have split, but a friend began to explain to us what was happening—that this was a manifestation of the power of the Holy Spirit.

We used to joke that perhaps we would have to go back to Notre Dame University to receive the baptism in the Holy Spirit, but that proved unnecessary. God answered our prayers by sending to our door one of the most unlikely persons in the world, a Trappist monk, from the monastery in nearby Vina.

The Trappists are one of the most cloistered orders in the Roman Catholic Church. They usually support themselves by farming. As it happened on this particular occasion, a part of a harvester had broken down. This created an emergency that called for an exception to the rule of remaining inside the monastery walls. Father Joseph was sent to Colusa to get this necessary part. He knew Yvonne and me very well because he was our spiritual director and confessor, and we used to visit him at the monastery on a regular basis.

No sooner had he sat down when Yvonne asked him, "Father Joe, what do you know about the baptism in the Holy Spirit?"

His countenance lit up with joy and he replied with animation.

"It's very interesting you should ask that. Last weekend, Pentecost Sunday, David Duplessis (a man called Mr. Pentecost), visited the monastery. As a result, the Abbott and ten of the monks were baptized in the Holy Spirit. Now the monastery is going to be opened to the public for a Life in the Spirit Seminar, a series of teachings on the baptism in the Holy Spirit by Father Dennis Bennett."

Another answer to our prayer had arrived.

Fascinated by how God seemed to be guiding us,

we attended the Life in the Spirit Seminar. On the last night, the monks prayed over us. I was still leery about the idea of letting go to the Holy Spirit. I had spent my life as a professional religious individual, always being in control. But when Brother Adam laid hands on me, I could feel the presence of Jesus. Because I knew that Brother Adam was a very trustworthy man, I was willing to accept his Holy Spirit. Even though nothing dramatic happened, I left with a deep peace infusing my body.

Later that night after Yvonne and I had gone to bed, she woke me up, saying that I had been talking in my sleep. It turned out to be my prayer language!—the same kind of spiritual language that the followers of Christ received on the day of Pentecost. (For a teaching on what we learned about the baptism of the Holy Spirit, please see Appendix I).

God's Mysterious Ways

After Yvonne and I were born again and filled with the Holy Spirit, God impressed two scriptures upon us: "Seek first the kingdom of God and His righteousness, and all these things shall be added to you" (Matthew 6:33 NKJV); and "My God shall supply all your need according to His riches in glory by Christ Jesus" (Philippians 4:19 NKJV).

Whenever we had a need, we wrote out a description of it and tucked the note in the Bible at one of those verses. To our delight, God honored His Word in many miraculous ways, providing for us both materially and spiritually.

Not only did He provide for us, but He began guiding us in new and mysterious ways. After several years as a probation officer in Colusa County, I got a job as Assistant Chief Probation Officer in another county some distance from Colusa. This meant selling our home in Colusa.

A volunteer helper at the probation office was the wife of a wealthy local rice farmer. Every once in awhile she would stop by our house and tell us that if we ever moved, she would like to buy our home. One evening, immediately following my interview for the new job, I got a phone call from this lady's husband asking how much I wanted for the house. I gave him my figure.

"That's fine with me," he responded. "Is cash okay? I'll meet you at the title company tomorrow morning at 9:00 a.m.."

Praise the Lord!

Thankful to God for this financial blessing, we moved to Red Bluff and rented a very nice four-bedroom home with a spacious living room and backyard pool. After several months of renting this house, the owner asked us to make an offer.   We made a very low one because that was all we could afford. Cutting through many complications, God created a way for us to assume the owner's loan at 4.5% interest. We purchased the house at approximately half the market value and ended up with a very low monthly mortgage payment.

But without my knowing it, my old tendency to be a workaholic began to creep back into my life. I became too busy to spend quality time alone with God or my family.   In the evenings I taught night school, but also finished up classes in graduate school. Weekends I spent at my office correcting papers or studying in preparation for class. I never stopped to think what I was doing to my precious wife and family who saw me only at mealtimes.   I shudder to think how oblivious I was to Yvonne's difficulties in raising our two small children, for our second daughter, Seana, had been born just prior to our move.

My blind ambition for career advancement made me insensitive to the needs of my wife and family. I became an emotionally absent husband and father. And like Jonah, I was running from God's calling on my life, getting sidetracked instead of listening to His will. Thanks be to God, He still had ways of getting through to me. Although my goal was to move from Assistant Chief to Chief Probation Officer, God had other ideas.

On Tuesday evenings, Yvonne and I were attending a prayer meeting of about three hundred people. At one point my boss, the Chief Probation Officer, expressed interest in going with me to this prayer meeting. The very first evening that he came, he went forward at the altar call and made Jesus Lord of his life.

On the way home he asked about the baptism of the Holy Spirit. I explained it to him and asked if he would like to receive the infilling of the Holy Spirit. He said he would. As we drove home along the freeway, I laid my hand on his head and he began speaking in tongues.

I was so excited to have another Christian in the office. Up to this point I had been doing spiritual warfare all alone just to survive a very difficult environment. Now I had a partner and the battle intensified, especially since the two of us agreed to pray together each morning for fifteen minutes before work time began.

Part of my job as Assistant Chief was to assign the court reports that were referred by the Superior Court Judge each week. The number of reports depended on how many cases came up for preliminary hearing on any particular week. Sometimes I had to assign each officer two to three reports on top of the ones from the previous week. At times this created tension, but the circumstances were beyond my control. I always tried to balance the workload as fairly as possible.

One day I assigned two or three reports to a particular officer. He blew up and began to rant and rave about my being unfair. I suspended this officer for three days, which infuriated him all the more. He went to the grand jury and filed a complaint against me, claiming that I had discriminated against him. He further accused me of correcting my college students' papers on county time.

At this time I was teaching an evening class and often used my office on weekends for studying or correcting papers. I made the mistake of keeping my books and the students' papers on my desk during the week. The complaint resulted in a grand jury investigation. Even though I was completely exonerated of wrongdoing, the damage had been done. Some of the staff sided with the complainant and the tension grew worse. I sought God fervently for His will in my life. As we prayed, Yvonne and I felt that we had heard from God that I should resign because He had other plans for my life.

It is interesting to note how God healed the relationship with the above-mentioned young man. Several years later when I was attending a Bill Gothard Seminar, this young man approached me.

"Vince," he said, "I'm asking your forgiveness for the way I acted toward you. I was wrong. Please forgive me."

"Of course, I forgive you," I said, hugging him. He shared that he had recently become a born-again Christian. To God be the glory!

I took a leap of faith and resigned my job at the probation department. When the part-time teaching job terminated at the end of the spring semester, I had no visible income of any kind. From my prayers, it seemed that God was calling me to a walk of faith in preparation for serving Him in full-time ministry. But I felt that my seminary Bible training was very inadequate. I wrestled with the idea of going to Bible school.

As I prayed more about this, God seemed to tell me to set aside a room in our home where I could spend each day studying the Bible, and that the Holy Spirit would teach and reveal the Word of God to me.

It wasn't all that easy, but Yvonne and I set out to follow God's instructions, trusting and obeying no matter how mysterious the pathway.

The Lord Provides

After my resignation, I turned the den into a place for studying God's Word. I began pouring over the Bible, discovering the richness of His message to us.

To survive financially, I was forced to draw out my retirement fund. We paid our bills with that money but had a considerable amount left over. God guided us to give away the remaining money to people who needed both a financial boost and a boost in their faith in Jehovah Jirah, their Provider.

God in turn provided for us month after month, as I studied for almost two years. We were a family of four with no visible source of income, but with the usual monthly bills to pay: mortgage, utilities, food, and clothing. We got by on about $800 a month because God had already arranged for a very low mortgage payment.

Some months we found that money had been deposited in our bank account but we never knew the source. God had obviously prompted someone to act on our behalf. Often, we received money in the mail. One day two envelopes arrived in the mail with the same handwriting on each. I opened one and found $80 in cash, wrapped in a piece of brown paper. I opened the second one and found a $5 bill wrapped in a similar piece of paper that read: "Whoops! God said $85, not $80."

When a bill came in, we would put it in the Bible,

usually at Matthew 6:33-34, "Seek ye first the kingdom of God and His righteousness; and all these things shall be added to you. Do not be anxious for tomorrow for tomorrow will take care of itself."

At one point we urgently needed $300 to make the house and car payment. That evening we wrote a note which went something like this: "Dear God, we need $300 by tomorrow. Thank you, Lord, for your faithfulness to your promise in Matthew 6:33 and Philippians 4:19."

Early next morning I was already in my study when the doorbell rang. Yvonne went to the door. A lady said, "One of these is from my mother," and handed Yvonne an envelope. Then she left. Yvonne brought the envelope to my study and we opened it to find two checks; one for $200 and one for $100. We rejoiced in God.

During this time we were holding a prayer meeting every Saturday evening in our home. Afterward we usually had a time of fellowship, eating the cookies, cakes and pies that people would bring.

One particular Saturday evening only two small pies were brought in for refreshments. Yvonne came to me wondering if we should just skip refreshments that evening. A boldness welled up inside me, and I found myself saying, "Let's use what God had provided." In the natural, I should have agreed with Yvonne, knowing that two small pies would not go very far among all these people. Later on we realized the miracle that God had worked. Everyone who wanted pie had some and there was plenty of pie left over. Praise the Lord!

On another occasion we needed $100 in a hurry. We followed the usual procedure of writing out our request and putting it in the Bible. This was mid-week. On Saturday, God provided $100 through five $20 bills that people had dropped off during the day. We were eager to share this testimony at the prayer meeting that evening.

As I shared, a man in the group began to weep. Kneeling in the middle of the room, he confessed, "Three days ago I felt God telling me to write a check for $100 to Vince and Yvonne." But I replied, "Lord, let someone else do it. Now I know I have missed a blessing that five people had to make up for."

I had been reading in the Bible about how God emphasizes giving in order to bless us spiritually. "It is more blessed to give than to receive" (Acts 20:35). "Give and it will be given unto you; good measure, pressed down, shaken together, running over, they will pour into your lap. For by your standard of measure it will be measured to you in return"(Luke 6:38).

Week after week God continued to meet our needs in surprising ways. One lady insisted that God had told her to do our grocery shopping each week. We felt very reluctant, knowing that the woman had an unemployed husband and four children. Yet in obedience to God, Yvonne gave her a list. We discovered that each week the lady brought us groceries, her family in turn was marvelously blessed.

Through this whole process of receiving gifts and provisions from others, God was dealing with my pride. Raised with the work ethic that the man is the breadwinner for his family, I chaffed at my inability to support my family. Yet every time a door opened for a job, it would close immediately. This happened several times to the point where I would get angry with God, in spite of His continuous provision.

I had to learn to swallow my pride when people were always bringing us food. Often I didn't even want to answer the door. One day, as I hesitated to answer the door, God impressed on me very clearly, not in an audible voice, yet very real, *Vince, there are people I want to bless through their giving, but in order to do this, I need people who are willing to receive.*

I immediately fell on my face and repented, saying "Here I am Lord, use me."

One time we wondered why the money did not come in to pay our mortgage and other bills. We were about two months in arrears when I received a phone call from the lending institution informing me that they were in the process of foreclosing on our home.

Faith rose up inside me and I heard myself saying, "Oh, I am sorry about that, but my Father seems to have delayed these payments for some reason."

"What does your father have to do with this?" she asked.

"My Father has been taking care of these payments all along," I answered. "If you knew Him, you wouldn't be concerned because my Father is a multi-millionaire and is faithful to His promises."

"I'm so sorry, sir, for bothering you," she apologized. "I'm sure it will be taken care of." She hung up before I had an opportunity to witness to her about my Father God, who owns all the gold and the silver in the world (Haggai 2:8) and all the cattle on a thousand hills (Psalm 50:10). God immediately provided sufficient funds to make up the past payments. Again, to God be the glory.

One of the first places where I was invited to give my testimony was a prayer group in the San Francisco Bay Area. During the meeting the leader, a friend of ours, had shared a powerful testimony of his own. On the previous Sunday evening, while he was ministering at a church in the Bay Area, God pointed out a lady at the back of the church and said to him, "That lady has a financial need and I want you to give her what you have in your wallet."

He went to the lady, opening his wallet as he approached her. He found two $20 bills. He pulled out a $20, gave it to the lady, and as he did, he heard a still small voice saying, *I said to give her all that you have in your wallet*. He hesitated and began to argue with God, saying, "Lord, that is all I have left for groceries." Then he heard the Lord say, *If you trust Me and obey, I will multiply one-hundred fold to you*. With that he parted with the other $20 bill.

The lady to whom he gave his money wept openly, saying how she had asked God that morning for $40. When the love offering was received for our friend that evening, there was a diamond ring in the offering basket. A note attached to the ring read, "This ring has been appraised at $4,000."

Soon after my friend had shared this testimony, a love offering was received. All I had in my wallet was $2.00. I knew that I had sufficient gas to get home, but I figured I needed to keep a couple of dollars in case of emergency. As the basket approached, I had the impression in my spirit that God was saying, *Trust Me and see Me do the same for you with a hundred-fold return*. With that, I plunked my last $2.00 into the basket, thinking that the offering was for my friend.

When the meeting was over, my friend put the offering into a paper bag. To my amazement, he turned to me and said, "I believe the Lord wants you to have this." I stuck the paper bag into my pocket and walked to my car to drive home. As I was pulling out of the parking lot, a lady came running up, waving her hands for me to stop.

I lowered the window.

"I must obey God," she exclaimed. "He told me to give you this." She handed me a check for $150.

I was flabbergasted, yet curious about what might be in the paper bag in my pocket. I counted it and sure enough, it contained $50 cash. That made a hundred-fold blessing from my original $2.00! I praised and thanked God all the way home.

Instrument of the Holy Spirit

As I surrendered my will and allowed God to have His way with me, I was soon ministering on a regular basis at Full Gospel Businessmen's banquets all over northern California. Remember the man that came to our door in Colusa with the book, *Nine O'Clock in the Morning*, and the tapes by the Ranaghans? That man, Harold Grimes, was a field representative for Full Gospel Businessmen's Fellowship International in northern California. He had happened to find out about us from the president of a local chapter.

At the same time Yvonne, who was a Women's Aglow area officer, was ministering at Women's Aglow meetings. Interestingly, when I ministered at Full Gospel meetings she was often asked to speak as well, and when Yvonne ministered at Aglow meetings, I was often asked to speak. This was contrary to the normal policy of both fellowships.

One evening in Las Cruces, New Mexico, I ministered at a FGBM banquet and the anointing of God for healing was very strong. A young lady's body was totally twisted by severe scoliosis. As I laid my hands on her and asked God to heal her, her body began to contort. She twisted back and forth for several minutes, and then was totally healed.

Prior to that meeting, I had ministered at a church in El Paso, Texas, which met in the civic center. My brother, a Roman Catholic priest who was living in Texas, came to that meeting. He came in just at the point where God was giving me great liberty to lead a fun song, "...and that's why I'm bananas for the Lord!"   My conservative brother was convinced that I was mixed up with a bunch of spiritual radicals. I reminded him that Jesus was pretty radical in His ministry.

Jesus tells us, "Truly truly I say to you, he who believes in Me, the works that I do shall he do also; and greater works than these shall he do; because I go to the Father" (John 14:12). This powerful scripture shows that every believer is called to continue the Lord's miracle ministry. What a shame that most of us have not taken Jesus at His word. Yet we know His Word is truth and that He cannot lie. Why do we hold back from releasing our faith in the miracle working power of God? I know it seems hard to grasp at times, but if we would only believe and allow ourselves to experience the truth of God's Word, we would see miracles as the norm and not the exception.

All it takes is the initial step of faith, knowing that God is calling us, as He called Peter to step out of the boat on the water. Peter did great as long as he kept his eyes on Jesus, but when he began to look at the circumstances—the waves around him—his faith wavered. We all need to take a lesson from Peter's experience. When praying for a person with cancer, it is easy to let that word "cancer" influence us. But think about it. Cancer, or any other serious disease, is no more difficult for God than a simple headache. By believing John 14:12 and acting upon it, what an impact we can make for the kingdom of God!

One Saturday evening, Yvonne and I spoke at a FGBMFI/Aglow combination banquet meeting. Afterward, we ministered separately, Yvonne to the women and I to the men. Two pastors requested me to come and minister at their church the next morning. I told them I would go to whichever church God would guide me to in prayer. Yvonne, likewise, received an invitation for us to visit a Roman Catholic church, but she did not tell me about it. She believed we would not be accepted to minister in a Roman Catholic church unless God specifically revealed it to me.

Before retiring for the night, we prayed for God's direction regarding which of the two invitations I should accept. Somehow I had no leading for either one. During the night, I kept waking up with the name of a town which I knew was in the general area of where we were staying, but it made no sense to me. In the morning, Yvonne asked me where we were going to minister. I told her I had no clear direction, but when I mentioned the name of the town that kept coming to my mind during the night, she jumped up and down, praising God, saying, "That's it! That's the name of the place where a lady asked me if we would visit her Catholic Church."

We both agreed that it had to be God at work, and so by faith, we decided to obey.

The lady met us as we pulled up outside the church. She greeted us excitedly with the news that the priest had just been taken by ambulance to the hospital with a heart attack. She said that we would need to minister. A lot of people were milling around outside the church, talking in low tones, obviously concerned for the welfare of their pastor. Others were inside the church on their knees praying for his recovery.

The lady pushed ahead of us through the crowd, announcing like a town crier of old, "God has brought us a priest." She knew our background from our testimony the previous night.

One would need a Roman Catholic background to

appreciate the irony of the situation in which we found ourselves. Perhaps comedy would be a better word. Here we were, my wife and I, walking arm-in-arm behind this lady who was shouting, "God brought us a priest." Maybe God blinded their eyes to the fact that I was not wearing the traditional black suit and clerical collar, and had a wedding ring on my finger, and a woman on my arm. Roman Catholic priests, as a rule, are not married. However, it is interesting to note that there is an unexplainable exception to this rule. An Episcopal priest who converts to Catholicism is allowed to minister as a Roman Catholic priest and remain married.

Yvonne and I sat in the front row waiting for God's confirmation that He wanted me to minister in this place and under these circumstances. Had the pastor been present, there was no way in the world that we would have been welcomed, much less allowed to minister.

As the lady ushered me into a back room to prepare for the Mass, I was a mess trying to figure out what to do. Yvonne remained seated in the front row, praying desperately for direction. The Bible on her lap fell to the floor. She picked it up and read where it had opened. She knew it was God's answer, because she felt God saying to her, *Show this passage to your husband.*

She brought me this scripture from Hebrews 7:12-19: "For when the priesthood is changed of necessity there takes place a change of law also. And this is clearer still, if another priest arises according to the likeness of Melchizedek, who has become such, not on the basis of a law of physical requirement, but according to the power of an indestructible life. For it is witnessed of him 'thou art a priest forever according to the order of Melchizedek.' For on the one hand, there is a setting aside of a former commandment because of its weakness and uselessness (for the law made nothing perfect), and on the other hand there is a bringing in of a better hope, through which we draw near to God."

With this confirmation from God's Word, I decided to go ahead and minister to the congregation. I read the Scripture assigned for that Sunday, where Jesus stresses the necessity of being born again. "Truly, truly, I say to you, unless one is born again, he cannot see the kingdom of God...Do not marvel that I said to you, 'You must be born again.'" (John 3:3,7).

Then I began to give a homily. Soon I felt the impression to stop.

Looking out at the people, I said, "God seems to be telling me that you do not know the meaning of this Bible verse about being born again." No one budged, but the still small voice of the Lord spoke within me. *They need to be born again.*

So I began explaining to the people that Christ's death on the cross paid the full price for a Divine pardon of our sins. Guiding them through Romans 3:19-26, I stressed verse 23, "For all have sinned and fall short of the glory of God." I pointed out that this passage shows the need for repentance.

Then I followed with the next step in God's plan of salvation. "If you confess with your mouth Jesus as Lord and believe in your heart that God raised him from the dead, you shall be saved; for with the heart man believes, resulting in righteousness, and with the mouth he confesses, resulting in salvation" (Romans 10:9-10).

I invited those to stand who wished to confess Jesus as their Lord and Savior. First a few stood, then more, until almost everyone was on their feet. I asked them to repeat after me, "Dear Jesus, I acknowledge that I am a sinner. I repent of every sin in my life. I receive the forgiveness You provided for me through Your shed blood on the cross of Calvary. I invite You to come into my life to be Lord of every area of my life, and I thank You."

That afternoon we had dinner with the family of the lady that had invited us to her church. She told us that the pastor had recovered well and was home from the hospital, only having had an attack of indigestion! Hallelujah! Obviously, had he been there that morning, we would not have had that glorious opportunity for those people to receive salvation. What an awesome experience to keep us mindful of the mighty God we serve.

Around this time I had the privilege of teaching at the annual FGBMFI convention. I had prepared for this assignment with much prayer and study. I was supposed to teach in the first session following the luncheon meeting where Demos Shekarian was the speaker. The lunch meeting went on and on, with testimony after testimony, before Demos began to speak.

I asked someone to call me when it was time for me to speak. Then I slipped out of the meeting and went to my room, where I paced back and forth. The word that God had given me was burning like fire in my spirit. As I paced I really identified with Jeremiah, who wrote, "In my heart it (the Word) becomes like a burning fire shut up in my bones; and I am weary of holding it in, and I cannot endure it" (Jeremiah 20:9). For the first time I was experiencing the message I had prepared exploding within me, wanting to be expressed. This was a far cry from the first half of my adult life as a priest, when Yvonne had rightly diagnosed my wooden, "going-through-the-motions" style as a lack of being filled with God's own Spirit.

When I was finally called, I entered the room full of expectant faces, and gave the message on my heart with full abandon to the power and passion coursing through my soul.

Signs and Wonders

In addition to speaking at Full Gospel Businessmen's banquets, I began to get invitations to teach Bible studies in neighboring communities. We had three weekly Bible studies in addition to a Saturday evening prayer meeting. At the end of each Bible study, we would have a time of prayer and just about every week somebody got saved, filled with the Holy Spirit, or healed. One of these Bible studies was in Paradise, California. It met on Monday evenings.

On Saturday evenings we opened our home to a prayer meeting that was the high point of each week. We saw God's wisdom of providing us with a spacious living room. We began each meeting with praise and worship, and kept praising and worshipping until the glorious presence of God filled the room. Sometimes the anointing was so strong that people could no longer remain standing and began to fall to the ground in His awesome presence.

One particular area where God began to use me was in the healing of upper and lower back problems. With lower back problems, I learned that when I compared both legs, one was usually shorter than the other. With a simple prayer asking God to minister to the person's need, the shorter leg would grow in front of our eyes, becoming even with the other and thereby solving the problem. With upper back problems, I found that as people would extend their arms forward, God would make the necessary adjustments as we prayed a simple prayer.

One evening, a lady with a severe back problem requested prayer not for herself, but for a friend who also had a very bad back problem. This unselfish lady sat in as proxy for her friend and received a miraculous healing for herself.

Many times, especially during the summer months, people who got saved at the prayer meeting would request water baptism. The pool in our backyard became a baptismal font, another sign of God's foresight in blessing us with this particular home. Often it was close to midnight before we got through with the prayer meeting and baptisms.

One time a young lady came to the prayer meeting and was gloriously saved. She insisted on being water baptized in the clothes that she had worn to the meeting. It was close to midnight when she left for home in her wet clothes. Knowing that her husband was not a Christian, my wife tried to get her to put on some dry clothes. We expected that her husband would never allow her to come back. But the following Saturday evening they both came and he too, was gloriously saved.

One night a teenage boy showed up at our door saying, "I need to get saved." He was not only saved, but filled with the Holy Spirit.

A prominent local law-enforcement officer came to our home asking, "I see something in your life that I want. What is it?"

We said, "It's Jesus."

"Then I want Jesus," he declared, "and all that He has for me."

The man began to grow spiritually as he received teaching and experienced the power of Jesus at work in the prayer meetings and in his life. Soon this officer began to experience an anointing as he ministered to others.

Almost every week at the prayer meeting he would give a testimony on how God had worked through him in marvelous ways during the previous week. One night on duty he turned around to find a gun leveled at his head.

He quietly said to his would-be assassin, "In the name of Jesus I command you to put down the gun."

Immediately the man dropped his gun and surrendered.

One day, three or four deputies were trying to arrest and handcuff a huge fellow, who kept tossing them off as though they were rag dolls. Our friend arrived on the scene as a backup and said to this big guy, "In the name of Jesus, put your hands behind your back." The suspect immediately obeyed and was handcuffed. You can imagine what kind of a witness these incidents were to law enforcement officers in that area.

After a season of being used in a healing ministry, God decided to teach me a lesson in humility.

I was invited to minister at a prayer group in a parish where I had previously served as associate priest. The lay leaders of the prayer group took advantage of the fact that their Irish priest was on vacation in Ireland. This priest had denounced me from the pulpit and had forbidden the people to attend any of my Bible studies or meetings. I saw this invitation as an opportunity to redeem my reputation.

On previous occasions God had used me in the healing of lower-back problems by lengthening peoples' shorter leg. God had been honoring this prayer in ninety percent of the cases. While I was waiting for the meeting to begin, I observed a man limping as he entered the room. My first reaction was, *A-hah, there is a healing that will impress everyone.*

After I had done some teaching and shared how God was honoring my prayers, especially for back problems, I asked if anyone needed prayer for this particular problem. A chair, called the "hot seat," was put in the middle of the circle and I decided to begin with this man I had noticed earlier.

As he didn't volunteer, I called him forward to sit in the hot seat. Then I asked the people to gather closely around and see God do a miracle. In truth, I was thinking, *see Vince do a miracle.* I knelt before the man and lifted his feet to see which leg was shorter. To my horror I discovered he had a wooden leg.

At that moment, the Lord helped me see my prideful motives. Though it felt terribly embarrassing, I told the people that my need to impress them was getting in the way of really listening to God's will. I repented on the spot and asked God's forgiveness. God was quick to respond to my newfound humility, and graciously continued to use me in a ministry of physical healing.

There was one other occasion prior to this incident when God had tried to teach me this same lesson in a much less conspicuous way, but I didn't learn from that experience.

I accompanied my wife to minister at a Women's Aglow meeting. As we were going into the meeting, there was a lady limping and using a cane.

I greeted her and said, "God is going to heal you today."

We had the meeting and many ladies came forward for ministry, but not this particular lady. When we were leaving the meeting, I again met this lady, but this time she had no cane and was walking normally.

I got all excited and said to her, "Praise the Lord, you're healed."

Her very calm response was, "Yes. Didn't you say that God was going to do it? Well, He did."

"Why didn't you come up in the healing line?" I asked.

"I didn't need to," she replied, "I was already healed."

This was the first time that pride had tried to enter in and God had dealt with it privately. However it took the incident with the wooden leg to learn the lesson of never attempting to usurp God's glory.

I learned that without humility I have difficulty fulfilling God's will for me. Jesus left us a very important scripture: "Learn from Me, for I am meek and humble of heart and you will find rest for your souls"(Matthew 11:29). Of all His virtues, humility is the only one that Jesus pointed out in Himself.

The opposite of humility is pride. Susceptibility to pride seems to be an inherent flaw in human nature since the time of Adam. Pride was the basic problem that caused Adam and Eve to sin by disobeying God. Through them we all inherited a sinful nature through the corruption of the human seed. Jesus was able to redeem the human race because He wasn't born of human seed, but was conceived by the power of the Holy Spirit (Luke1:35).

Consider this parable told by Jesus: "Two men went up into the temple to pray, one a Pharisee, the other a tax gatherer. The Pharisee stood and was praying thus to himself, 'God, I thank Thee that I am not like other people; swindlers, unjust, adulterers, or even like this tax gatherer. I fast twice a week, I pay tithes of all that I get.' But the tax gatherer, standing some distance away, was even unwilling to lift up his eyes to heaven, but was beating his breast, saying, 'God, be merciful to me, the sinner.' I tell you, this man went down to his house justified rather than the other; for everyone who exalts himself shall be humbled, but he who humbles himself shall be exalted" (Luke 18:10-14).

The Pharisee set himself above the other man, boasting about his good works. The humble man prayed, "God be merciful to me, a sinner."

Coming Out

During the first part of our two-year walk of faith, we were still involved in the Catholic church. I had preached for sixteen years that it was a mortal sin to miss Mass on Sunday unless one were seriously ill. On Sunday mornings Yvonne and I still felt obliged to attend Mass. Then forty-five minutes later we would come away with an empty feeling.

One Sunday morning following Mass, we were so spiritually dry that we decided we needed to get some spiritual food. We went to the local Assembly of God Church, where we were fed the Word of God, preached by a precious pastor who became a dear friend.

We continued going to the Assembly of God church for about a year. On Saturday evenings, we ministered to the people at the prayer meeting in our home, many of whom were Catholics, and on Sunday morning we received ministry from our Assembly of God pastor friend, but only after we had fulfilled our "obligation" of attending Mass.

Believe me, it is not easy to break away from traditions that have been pounded into one's head from childhood. There are some elderly Catholics today who will not eat meat on Friday because as children they were taught it was a mortal sin.

Interestingly, God showed me while I was still a priest the silliness of this "no meat on Friday under penalty of mortal sin" idea.

When I had served the Catholic Church as an associate pastor at a parish next the state fair grounds, I had observed how the local bishop would give a dispensation to Catholics within the fair grounds to eat meat on the Friday during the state fair.

Imagine this scenario. Two brothers have between them only enough money for one hot dog. One brother enters the fairgrounds and buys a hot dog. He trots over to the cyclone fence, where his little brother waits outside. He pushes the hot dog through the fence for his little brother to take a bite. Now the brother on the outside has committed a mortal sin because he is outside the fence, but the one on the inside is without sin. Oh, the folly of religious legalism!

Many Catholics came to the Saturday evening prayer meeting in our home. Two evangelist friends with Catholic backgrounds sometimes showed up to help us out. Both Ed and Bill moved powerfully in the gift of the word of knowledge, a manifestation of the Holy Spirit in which God reveals supernatural knowledge to help or encourage someone.

Ed would walk people around the block as God revealed to him the problems they were having in their life. Some of them who did not understand how the word of knowledge worked accused us of telling Ed about their problems saying, "Why did you tell him about us?" Of course, we had not told him anything.

Bill also moved in the gifts of the Holy Spirit.

When either one of these men ministered at the Saturday evening prayer meeting, they would stay overnight, and most of the people would return for a meeting on Sunday morning. Many of them were Roman Catholics who had fulfilled their Mass obligation on Saturday evening.

One Saturday evening, about one year into our

two-year faith walk, Bill was ministering at the prayer meeting when he began to give a message in tongues with interpretation. The Apostle Paul describes this gift of the Spirit in the first book to the Corinthians. Standing before Yvonne and me, Bill prophesied over us: "Behold I have called you to be My shepherds and to feed My people on the Lord's Day."

To us this clearly meant having a service on Sunday morning. We immediately began to question this message.

"Bill," I protested, "There is no way we can do this. We are deeply involved in the local parish and this would mean breaking ranks with my friend, Father Mike. Not only that, we feel called to evangelize from within the local Catholic parish."

With that, Bill began to speak once more in tongues with interpretation saying, "The Lord is asking me to ask you a simple question. How many people have you led to salvation through your parish ministry?"

Yvonne and I looked at each other and shook our heads saying, "None that we know of."

Again Bill spoke in tongues with interpretation saying, "Now the Lord is asking me to ask you how many people have been led to salvation through ministry from your home?"

All we could respond was, "Many, many people."

At this point Bill added his own commentary saying, "Now do you two understand what God is trying to communicate to you?"

Hesitantly, we had to admit we understood God wanted us to open our home for ministry on Sunday mornings.

The next morning most of the people from the previous evening returned to hear Bill preach, as was the custom of the visiting evangelist. We began with the usual praise and worship portion of the service. Then it was time for the visiting minister to bring the message. We were all waiting in silence for Bill to begin, but he showed no signs of getting started.

Finally, I caught his eye and said, "Bill, aren't you going to bring us the message?"

His response was, "Not me, Vince. Didn't you hear God speak to you last night? You are called to pastor this group and bring the message."

My knees knocked together with fright and my Bible fell to the floor. I picked it up where it had opened—at John 15—and took this as a sign that God wanted me to teach from this chapter.

As I began to read I felt the anointing of God come upon me in a wonderful way and the words began to flow from my lips. This was the first time that I preached under such a strong anointing of the Holy Spirit. It was exhilarating.

To this day, John 15 , where Jesus describes Himself as the true Vine and tells us to abide in Him, is a very significant portion of Scripture for me. "As the Father loved Me," Jesus says, "I also have loved you; abide in My love."

The Truth That Set Us Free

Since God was now requiring that we meet on Sunday mornings, this meant we were no longer just a prayer group. We had matured into a fellowship. We called ourselves Spiritual Renewal Fellowship, and affiliated the group under the covering of a church in the San Francisco Bay Area. By pastoring Spiritual Renewal Fellowship, Yvonne and I gave up our last link with the Catholic Church.

This created a problem for many of the Catholics in the group, who decided to take their leave. The Catholics who remained were intent on studying the Bible for themselves and not having the Scriptures interpreted to them by Rome. One of the first requests I got was to do some teaching on the relationship of Roman Catholic doctrine with the Bible. As I began digging into the Word of God, I found that many Catholic teachings did not line up with the Bible.

For example, in 2 Timothy 2:5, the Word of God tells us: "There is one God and one mediator also between God and men, the man Christ Jesus." This means the Roman Catholic teaching that Mary is a mediator between God and man is unscriptural. So are the practices of praying to the saints and having priests offer masses to mediate between God and people.

All of this came as a shock, but the Word of God is very clear on this matter. The fellowship was committed to believing God's Word over the traditions of the church. We were submitting our lives to Jesus and His Word, not to any religious institution. "No man can serve two masters," said Jesus in Matthew 6:24.

Each time the truth of God's Word was clearly revealed to us, we believed because we knew that His Word was our final authority.

Our Catholic background made it difficult to root out and give up all our sacred cows. But the grace of God kept edifying us as we prayed for "the spirit of wisdom and revelation in the knowledge of Him, that the eyes of our understanding would be enlightened so we would know what was the hope of His calling and the riches of the glory of His inheritance in the saints" (Ephesians 1:17-18). Truly, we were Christ's heirs—His born again, Spirit-filled children.

We studied the Epistles of Peter and discovered that Christians are "a chosen race, a royal priesthood, a holy nation, a people for God's own possession that we may proclaim the excellencies of Him who has called us out of darkness into His marvelous light" (1 Peter 1:9).

In studying Hebrews we learned that Christ's work of redemption was finished once and for all on Calvary's cross. This meant that the Mass as a continuing sacrifice of Jesus on the cross of Calvary was unscriptural. "By this, (the sacrifice of Jesus on the cross) we have been sanctified through the offering of the body of Jesus Christ, once and for all...For by one offering, He has perfected for all time those who are sanctified" (Hebrews 10:10, 14).

Matthew 6:7 pretty well took care of the repetition of the rosary: "When you pray, do not (multiply words, repeating the same ones over and over, and) heap up phrases as the Gentiles do, for they think they will be heard for their much speaking" (Amplified).

Another Roman Catholic tradition was exposed in

the light of God's Word when I saw how the Ten Commandments are listed in Exodus 20 in the authorized version of the Bible. The first commandment is listed in verses 2 and 3; the second commandment in verses 4 and 5. Verse 4 reads as follows: "Thou shalt not make unto thee any graven image or likeness of anything that is in the heaven above or that is in the earth beneath, or that is in the water under the earth." Verse 5 says: "Thou shalt not bow down thyself to them."

The Roman Catholic Church omits the second commandment in Exodus 20, verses 4 and 5, but comes up with ten commandments by making two commandments out of number 10, and calling these the ninth and tenth commandments. In Exodus 20:17, of the authorized version of the Bible, the tenth commandment is as follows: "Thou shalt not covet thy neighbor's house, thou shalt not covet thy neighbor's wife, nor his manservant, nor his maidservant, nor his ox, nor his ass, nor anything that is thine neighbor's."

The Catholic Church lists its ninth commandment as, "You shall not covet your neighbor's wife," and the tenth commandment as, "You shall not covet your neighbor's goods."

Why has the Catholic Church omitted the second commandment as stated in Exodus 20:4-5? It would appear that the tradition of the Roman Catholic Church has in this case superseded Scripture, the Word of God, since the Catholic Church has long approved statues and religious objects for veneration and for sale.

In studying the history of the Roman Catholic Church, one finds that in 1854, Pope Pius IX established the doctrine of the Immaculate Conception. This meant that Mary was conceived and preserved immune from all stain of original sin. As a new doctrine, it entailed belief by all the faithful. Many Catholics and non-Catholics believe that the Immaculate Conception refers to Mary's conception of Jesus through the power of the Holy Spirit.

We know from Scripture that Jesus was sinless at all stages of His life from conception, because He was not born of the Adamic seed. "And the angel said to her, 'Do not be afraid, Mary, for you have found favor with God. And behold you will conceive in your womb and bear a son and you shall name Him Jesus. He shall be great and will be called the Son of the Most High and the Lord God will give Him the throne of His father David and He will reign over the house of Jacob forever and His kingdom will have no end.' Mary said to the angel, 'How can this be since I am a virgin?' And the angel answered and said to her, 'The Holy Spirit will come upon you and the power of the Most High will overshadow you; and for that reason the holy offspring shall be called the Son of God'" (Luke 1:30-35).

According to Roman Catholic teaching the Immaculate Conception means that when Mary was conceived in the womb of her mother in the natural way, unlike everybody else born of the seed of Adam, she did not inherit the stain of original sin, and that at no point in her life did she ever sin. This doctrine goes directly against the scriptures: "There is none righteous, not even one...All have sinned and fall short of the glory of God" (Romans 3:10, 23). "All" here means all human beings descended from the corrupted seed of Adam, and that includes Mary.

The doctrine of the Immaculate Conception poses another problem which came to light after it had been decreed, and became a "sticky wicket" for almost a century in the Roman Catholic Church. Romans 6:23 states, "For the wages of sin is death." From this we must conclude that one who had no sin should not die. The problem is if Mary had no sin, then she should not die. Also, if she had never sinned, then she did not need a Redeemer. Yet, we have in her own words: "My soul exalts the Lord, and my spirit has rejoiced in God my Savior" (Luke 1:46-47). Here we find Mary stating that she needed a Savior.

This dilemma baffled the Catholic Church for almost a century. Then in 1950 Pope Pius XII came up with a brilliant theory to settle the tormenting question. Unfortunately, there is absolutely no scriptural foundation for his theory. Still, a papal proclamation was issued enunciating a dogma of faith known as the Assumption of Mary—that God took Mary bodily and alive into heaven.

In our studies of the Bible we found that the Roman Catholic Church does not give clear scriptural teaching on how people are to receive salvation through their new birth in Christ. Catholics do not, for the most part, know how to have absolute assurance of salvation. They are hindered from perceiving that salvation is a free gift of God, and that all they need to do is believe in their hearts, confess with their lips, and embrace the good news that Jesus paid in full for their salvation on Calvary's cross.

The Apostle Paul sums up the very heart of the gospel—the finished work of salvation on Calvary—which is the basis of Christianity. "For I passed on to you first of all what I had also received, that Christ, the Messiah, the anointed one, died for our sins in accordance with (what) the Scriptures foretold, that He was buried, that He arose on the third day as the Scriptures foretold" (1 Corinthians 15: 3-4 Amplified version). Paul emphasizes that "If you confess with your mouth Jesus as Lord, and believe in your heart that God raised Him from the dead, you shall be saved. For with the heart man believes, resulting in righteousness, and with the mouth he confesses, resulting in salvation" (Romans 10:9-10).

The Roman Catholic Church teaches salvation through man's own efforts, leading a good life and doing penance for one's sins. That implies Jesus did not pay in full for our salvation with His shed blood on Calvary's cross. But Paul declares that salvation is a free gift of God, received by faith alone: "For by grace you are saved through faith, and that not of yourselves, it is a gift of God, not as a result of works, lest anyone should boast" (Ephesians 2:8-9).

Biblical Challenges
to Old Beliefs

The teaching authority of the Roman Catholic Church is called the magisterium, from the Latin word for master. The magisterium consists of the Pope who is the Bishop of Rome, together with all of the bishops. The magisterium claims infallibility. The doctrine of the infallibility of the Pope was defined in 1870 at the First Vatican Council under Pope Pius IX. When the arguments for infallibility were first presented, a great controversy ensued, culminating in the bishops' rejection of several drafts. Finally, a majority of the bishops were brought into line and the doctrine was approved.

This doctrine states that the pope is infallible, that is, divinely protected from error in his official teaching regarding faith and morals when he speaks *ex cathedra* (from the chair as supreme teacher of the Church). The First Vatican Council announced that, "We teach and define as divinely revealed that when the Roman Pontiff speaks *ex cathedra,* that is, when, in the exercise of his office as shepherd and teacher of all Christians, in virtue of his supreme apostolic authority, he defines a doctrine concerning faith or morals to be held by the whole Church, he possesses, by the divine assistance promised to him, in blessed Peter, that infallibility which the divine Redeemer willed His Church to enjoy in defining doctrine concerning faith and morals."

This decision became binding upon all Catholics everywhere—*Roma locuta est; causa finita est*—Rome has spoken; the case is closed.

The doctrine of infallibility was restated by the Second Vatican Council over half a century later. "The Roman Pontiff, head of the College of Bishops, enjoys this infallibility in virtue of his office, when, as supreme pastor and teacher of all the faithful... he proclaims in an absolute decision a doctrine pertaining to faith or morals. For that reason, his definitions are rightly said to be irreformable by their very nature and not by reason of the assent of the church, inasmuch as they were made with the assistance of the Holy Spirit promised to him in the person of blessed Peter himself; and as a consequence, they are in no way in need of the approval of others, and do not admit of appeal to any other tribunal."

Even though the pope may not be making an infallible decree, Catholics are still expected to obey without question. "This loyal submission of the will and intellect must be given, in a special way, to the authentic teaching authority of the Roman Pontiff, even when he does not speak *ex cathedra* in such wise, indeed, that his supreme teaching authority be acknowledged with respect, and that one sincerely adhere to decisions made by him" (Second Vatican Council).

Nevertheless, many Catholics today pick and choose for themselves what they want to believe. Jim McCarthy, in his book, *The Gospel According to Rome,* quotes how someone expresses this trend among Catholics today: "I'm Catholic by *my* definition, which is the only one that counts."

Fortunately, many Catholics are prayerfully

reading the Bible for themselves and finding that Roman Catholic doctrine in many instances is not what the Bible teaches. The Apostle John taught the early Christians to be suspicious of anyone who claimed to speak for God: "Beloved do not believe every spirit, but test the spirits to see whether they are from God; because many false prophets have gone out into the world" (I John 4:1).

From the Scriptures we know that the Holy Spirit is the Christian's infallible and authoritative teacher. Jesus tells us, "But when He, the Spirit of truth comes, He will guide you into all the truth; for He will not speak on His own initiative, but whatever He hears, He will speak; and He will disclose to you what is to come. He shall glorify Me; for He shall take of Mine and disclose it to you. All things that the Father has are Mine; therefore, I said, that He takes of Mine, and will disclose it to you" (John 16:13-15).

The claim to infallibility of the Roman Catholic Church rests upon three beliefs:

1. That Jesus made Peter head of the apostles and of the universal church.

2. That the apostles appointed bishops as their successors.

3. That the pope, as bishop of Rome, is Peter's successor.

But none of these claims can be established from Scripture. First, Jesus, not Peter, is the head of the apostles and the universal church. "And He is before all things and in Him all things hold together. He is also head of the body, the church, and He is the beginning, the first born from the dead so that He Himself might come to have first place in everything" (Colossians 1:17-18).

Although the Roman Catholic Church agrees that Scripture teaches Christ is the head of the church, it still insists that the pope is the visible head of the church, as declared in the First Vatican Council in 1870: "The Roman Pontiff is the successor of blessed Peter, the prince of the apostles, true vicar of Christ, head of the whole church, and father and teacher of all Christian people. To him, in blessed Peter, full power has been given by our Lord Jesus Christ to tend, rule and govern the universal church."

This claim rests upon the Roman Catholic Church interpretation of Matthew 16:18: "And I also say to you that you are Peter, and upon this rock I will build my church; and the gates of hell shall not overpower it." This is one of the few verses that Catholics can quote because it has been drilled into them from childhood that this verse contains strong biblical support for the Roman hierarchical system. Most Catholics have taken this for granted without searching Scripture for themselves, where they would find that this verse has nothing to do with the Roman Catholic pope and bishops.

The Roman Catholic Church interprets Jesus here to say, "You are Peter and upon 'you', Peter, I will build my church." Peter, it is held, was to be the rock upon which the Church would be built and therefore head of the apostles and visible head of the universal church.

There are several problems with this interpretation, as Jesus' choice of words here is very significant. Although Peter's name means rock (Petros), Jesus did not say, "You are Peter (Petros) and upon this rock (petros) I will build my church." What he did say was, "You are Peter (petros) and upon this rock (petra) I will build my church." The word Jesus used for rock is "petra", a feminine noun that refers to a mass of rock or bedrock. We find the same word in Matthew 7:24:25

86

and 27:60. Peter's name, on the other hand, is "Petros," a masculine gender word referring to a detached stone or small stone.

What Jesus is really saying to Peter is: "You are a stone and upon this bedrock I will build my church." Therefore, the bedrock upon which the church was to be built was something other than Peter.

To find this bedrock to which Jesus was referring, we need to go to the context, which the Roman Catholic church ignores. There is a very wise proverb which says, "A text without its context is a pretext." The context in Matthew 16:13-17 is not about Peter, but about Jesus and His identity. Jesus asked His disciples: "Who do men (people) say that I the son of man am? And they said 'Some say John the Baptist; some Elijah; and others Jeremiah, or one of the prophets.' He said to them, 'But who do you say that I am?' And Simon Peter answered and said, 'Thou are the Christ, the son of the living God.' And Jesus answered and said to him, 'Blessed are you Simon Barjona, because flesh and blood did not reveal this to you, but My Father who is in heaven.'"

Jesus is saying that Peter's understanding of Jesus' true identity was a direct revelation from God, and it was only at this point that Jesus states in verse 18: "Upon this bedrock" (petra), that is, the revelation of who Jesus really is, "I will build my church." In other words, the Lord Jesus as the Christ, the Son of the living God, was the bedrock foundation upon which His church would rest.

Peter writes, "For this is contained in Scripture: 'Behold I lay in Zion a choice stone, a precious cornerstone, and he who believes in Him shall not be disappointed. This precious value, then, is for you who believe, but for those who disbelieve, "The stone which the builders rejected, this became the very cornerstone," and "a stone of stumbling and a rock of offense;" for they stumble because they are disobedient to the word, and to this doom they were also appointed" (I Peter 2:6-8).

There are several other Old Testament Scriptures that support the interpretation of the rock (petra) as a symbol of God: I Samuel 2:2, Psalm 18:31, and Isaiah 44:8, to mention a few. It is significant that in Scripture, we never find the word *Petra* used symbolically of man, but only of God. There are many New Testament scriptures where Paul states that Christ is the one foundation upon which the church is built: "For no man can lay a foundation other than the one which is laid, which is Jesus Christ" (1 Cor. 3:11). When the Holy Spirit inspired the Greek text of the New Testament, the distinction between Peter as *petros,* and the rock as *petra,* was preserved in the context of the scriptural passage.

What about another verse that is so often quoted by the Roman Catholic Church? "I will give you the keys of the kingdom of heaven; and whatever you shall bind on earth shall have been bound in heaven, and whatever you shall loose on earth shall have been loosed in heaven" (Matthew 16:19). This verse is used by the Roman Catholic Church to try to prove that Peter was the head of the apostles and the universal church. Undoubtedly, keys may symbolize authority, but since no other verses supports the claim that Peter exercised supreme authority over the apostles or the church, this interpretation must be rejected since Scripture always supports Scripture.

What sort of authority is supported for Peter in the Bible? He is given the same authority as the other disciples—to bind and to loose (Matthew 18:18) in matters of church discipline.

There is no Biblical evidence that Peter ruled the apostles or had supreme authority over the early church. Neither was Peter the spokesman for the early apostles. On one occasion, Jesus had to rebuke Peter's impetuosity, saying, "Get thee behind me, Satan. You are a stumbling block to me; for you are not setting your mind on God's interests, but on man's" (Matthew 16:23). It is very significant to note that it was James, not Peter, who made the final definitive statement at the Council of Jerusalem: "Brethren, listen to me....Therefore, it is my judgment..." (Acts 15:13,19). And on another occasion Paul rebuked Peter openly for sitting with the Jews at a particular meal, and thereby showing favoritism.

Finally, the Pope is not Peter's successor. There is not a single Scriptural argument to substantiate this claim that the bishop of Rome, the Pope, is Peter's successor. The claim is based solely on human reasoning and conjecture.

It is not my purpose to go into the history of the papacy in order to cover this subject adequately. You can read for yourself the history of the papacy, which includes a thirty-nine-year period called the *Great Schism*, where several men claimed the title of Pope at the same time. In fact, even Roman Catholic scholars identify over thirty different men throughout the history of the church as anti-popes or false claimants.

I want to also express my experience that many Catholic lay people, religious, and priests love the Lord Jesus Christ very sincerely. In fact, a great many Catholics are serving Christ through the power of the Holy Spirit in the Catholic charismatic renewal. Unlike Yvonne and myself, they are comfortable remaining in the Catholic church.

A married couple whom Yvonne and I recently

met have a writing ministry to about thirty million Christians throughout the world. Dan and Katie Montgomery are presenting a Christ-centered, Spirit-filled, and Bible-based message to both Evangelicals and Catholics alike. Two of the many books they have written are *Beauty In The Stone: How God Sculpts You into the Image of Christ* (Thomas Nelson) and *God In Your Personality* (Pauline Books).

Paradise Found

Yvonne and I were leading Bible studies in three different communities. The one that grew the quickest was in Paradise, sixty miles from our home. We soon had thirty to forty people attending this meeting every Monday evening. We began this particular study in January—not the best month of the year to be traveling one hundred and twenty miles round trip. But by the grace of God, we always made it there—rain, hail, or snow. At times we literally prayed our way through the rough weather.

On one occasion, it was pouring rain. I was about to phone Paradise to say I could not make it that evening, when suddenly faith rose within me to go. As I drove through the storm, I prayed, "Father God, I have heard of you making a clear way for Your people through a storm. Please do that for me this evening." For the rest of my journey the thrashing rain stayed about ten feet ahead of me. I don't know how God did this, but I kept praising Him for His traveling mercies!

Psalm 91 became one of my favorite verses as a prayer of protection: "He who dwells in the secret place of the Most High shall remain stable and fixed under the shadow of the Almighty (whose power no foe can withstand). He will cover you with His pinions (feathers) and under His wings shall you trust and find refuge; His truth and His faithfulness are a shield and a buckler. You shall not be afraid of the terror of the night, nor of the arrow that flies by day" (Psalm 91:1,4-5, Amplified).

There are many testimonies of the power of this Psalm as a prayer for protection.

One in particular was given by a young lady who had just started attending a weekly Bible study. That evening the study was on Psalm 91. Following the Bible study, she was walking to her car which was parked on a dark street. A man grabbed her and started dragging her into the bushes. She panicked, but remembered Psalm 91:4.

She cried out, "O, God, cover me with your feathers," and kept repeating the word, "feathers, feathers, feathers!"

"You're crazy!" her attacker exclaimed, and ran off.

A young soldier was on the front lines of fierce fighting in the Viet Nam War. As his buddies were being mowed down all around him in a hail of bullets, this young Christian, who had memorized Psalm 91, prayed verse 7: "A thousand may fall at your side and ten thousand at your right hand; but it shall not approach you." Suddenly, he was knocked back by a bullet that hit him in the chest, but he was not injured. Upon examining his chest, he found that a bullet had pierced the little New Testament in his shirt pocket, making a hole through it as far as Psalm 91, where it stopped.

Oh, the power of God's Word! He is truly our shield and our buckler, our protection in the time of need.

Following the Monday night Bible study in Paradise each week, we had a time of prayer for the needs of those present. We saw God move mightily to touch many areas of need, both physical and spiritual. Broken bodies and broken relationships were restored, lives were changed, and bondage broken in the power of Jesus' name.

After a year of meeting weekly, the people had bonded together so closely that they began to express a desire to form a fellowship. At this time Yvonne and I were still holding the Spiritual Renewal Fellowship on Sunday mornings in our home. Some of the Paradise folks were making the hundred and twenty mile round trip each week. This showed us the depth of their commitment.

In the late fall of that year, an incident occurred that was devastating to our home fellowship. On some weekends, Yvonne and I had invitations for outside ministry. We accepted about one a month, and would be gone from our home fellowship over the weekend. When this happened we needed someone to fill in for us. In the summer of that year, a former pastor from southern California started attending our fellowship. He told a story of the unfair way that he had lost his pastorate in southern California. I had accepted his story without checking any further into his background. When he had been with us a few months, I began to let him fill in for us when we were ministering out of town.

One weekend we returned from ministering out of town and discovered that he had stolen most of the little flock to meet in his own home. Only a handful remained, which included those who came from Paradise.

These people began to request that we come to Paradise for Sunday services in addition to our Monday evening Bible study. After all, we had about forty people in the Paradise Bible study group who desired to form a fellowship.

Yvonne and I prayed and agreed that if by year's end God would plant the remaining people from our home fellowship in a good Bible teaching church, we would consider moving to Paradise.

The first Sunday service we held in Paradise found God drawing over fifty people together at the Veteran's Hall. We purposely did not try to promote our meetings so that the Holy Spirit would draw whomsoever He desired. The following Sunday there were approximately seventy people. Each Sunday the attendance increased a little more. By March we needed to find a bigger place to meet.

Our Paradise services were held on Sunday afternoon at 2:00 p.m. Following the service Yvonne and I were usually invited to someone's home for dinner. One Sunday evening our dinner host, Bob, informed us that he had heard of a church for rent or sale on the west end of town. After dinner, Bob and I headed out to find this church. As the side door of the church was unlocked, we peeked in to see a beautiful little sanctuary with white theater seats. We knocked on the office door and a man greeted us warmly. We told him that we had heard that the church was for sale or rent.

"Yes," he said, "it was until I moved in last week to begin a new work here. My wife is back east trying to get our home sold." We prayed with him and wished him well.

As we were leaving I said to Bob, "When we were on our way here, I felt that God was saying this is the place I have for you, but I guess I missed it."

"You didn't miss it, Vince," Bob replied. "I believe in my spirit that this is the place God has for us." Then he gave a word of knowledge: "This man's wife is not in agreement with him and is refusing to join him. He will be gone back home within two weeks." And so it happened.

We contacted the people responsible for the sale and found that they already had an offer which they were willing to accept. But there was still hope, as the deal was not yet finalized. They said they would know by the following Sunday and that they would attend our afternoon service.

When we arrived at the VFW hall the following Sunday, Palm Sunday, they greeted us saying, "The church is yours if you want it." They invited us to come and join them at the church for their final service that evening.

After they showed us around, we explained to them that we only had $1,000 for a down payment, but that we could make small monthly payments. At that time, the real estate interest rate was up to 15%. But these good people arranged for us to take over their monthly payments at 7%. Our first service in our new sanctuary was held the following Sunday, Resurrection Sunday. In one year we had grown to approximately two hundred people who really packed our little sanctuary. We named the congregation Paradise Christian Center.

The Irish Connection

At the beginning of our ministry at Paradise Christian Center, Yvonne and I had been married just under ten years, and had not yet visited my family in Ireland. One can hardly begin to imagine the shock to my family and the emotional devastation caused by the news of my leaving the priesthood and marrying Yvonne.

When I had originally written to my family to tell them of my decision to leave the priesthood, I did not share my intention to get married. In fact, I did not share this until after our marriage.

When my family finally found out, their feelings ran the gamut. Betrayal. Humiliation. Anger. I believe that the basis for their reaction was their fierce Irish pride. The big concern was "What will people think? What will people say?"

My sister Nora and her daughter Vera were the first members of the family to visit us in America and meet Yvonne. Nora was the sibling to whom I always felt the closest, perhaps because when I was a tot she took care of me on a regular basis. One of my earliest memories is of Nora pushing me in a baby buggy up to the top of a grassy knoll that led to a cemetery near our home. Perhaps it was wildflower season. Anyhow, Nora got distracted and soon the buggy and I were bumping down the hill, finally capsizing. I don't know whether it was the excitement or the trauma, but I'll never forget that wild ride!

Another time Nora took me to stay for a couple of days at Aunt Kate's. When Nora departed for home after delivering me, I got very upset and cried, "I'm lonesome after Nora. I want to go home to Nora." I think they may have had to take me home to Nora.

Nora and Vera came to visit us in our fourth year of marriage. Our daughter Kelly Ann was three years old and Yvonne was pregnant with Seana Marie. We had a great visit over a period of three weeks, showing them the beautiful sights of northern California.

Later, after Nora broke the ice, some other family members came to visit us, including my nephew Tony White, and my niece Geraldine with her husband Donal Kerr. I remember Tony's visit was in the month of October because we were amazed to find that the cool weather did not keep him out of the swimming pool. His response to our amazement was, "This is good swimming weather in Ireland."

On another occasion my niece, Ide O'Shaughnessy, and her friend Carole managed on a very tight budget to come and see us. We had a wonderful visit with these two vibrant lassies. Being Catholics, the worship at Paradise Christian Center seemed foreign to them, so they went to Mass on Sundays. However, Yvonne's sister Margie and her husband Larry witnessed to the girls about the message of salvation at every opportunity. To our delight, both girls were very open to the Gospel and invited Jesus to be Lord of their lives. We still have a piece of paper with the date of their commitment to Jesus.

The only downside was that when they returned to Ireland, there seemed to be no place where they could be discipled in the Word of God. If it were today, it would be a different story, as there are many home fellowships now in Ireland.

On one of my visits to Ireland, I mentioned about Ide's commitment while visiting us. "Yes," quipped a family member. "She got brainwashed and had to be de-programmed." How does one de-program a commitment to Jesus?

The most recent family members to visit us were my brother John, his wife Nora, and their daughter Mary. John was interested in the farming methods of California, but he seemed even more intent on finding out where Yvonne and I were religion-wise. His big question was, "What are you? If you are not Catholic, you must be Protestant."

"John," I said, "We're not Protestants. We are not protesting against anything or anyone. We are born again Christians, followers of Jesus Christ." I went on to explain that I view true Christianity as based on a personal relationship with Jesus, and not on any kind of religion. Religion is man-made, whereas Christianity is Christ-made, as we see in the Gospels.

John, who was a very intelligent person, liked to analyze what he read, so he had many questions about the Bible. Hopefully, we answered them satisfactorily. He seemed very open to receive truth, and took home several tracts that explained the message of salvation.

By the time of Yvonne's first visit to Ireland, we were welcomed with open arms and love.

My family loved Yvonne, which is not hard to do. As the saying goes, they rolled out the red carpet for us and we had a wonderful time. My only regret was that I had missed the growing up of many of my nieces and nephews over the previous ten years.

Nora and her husband Michael took us on many sight-seeing trips, as did other members of the family. We toured the west, the south, and the east portions of the scenic Emerald Isle, but we stayed away from the troubles of the north.

Those of us who have been gone from Ireland for many years have a renewed appreciation for the culture, beauty, and history of the Emerald Isle. St. Patrick, did much to Christianize Ireland. *The Confessions of St. Patrick*, reveal that he was a "born again" Christian.

A School Is Born

Once Paradise Christian Center was launched, both Yvonne and I were impressed with a vision for a Christian day school. We enjoyed being around children. I felt energized in their company, and young at heart. We began praying for the fulfillment of this vision for a school with grades K through 12. We began setting money aside toward that goal. With a lot of prayer and sacrifices on the part of many people, the vision became a reality by the end of our second year in Paradise.

On opening day we had sixty students. But the school was only in operation about one week when the town-planning director sent us a letter telling us to close down, claiming we were not zoned for a school.

I took the letter and went on my face before God. In my spirit I heard Isaiah 54:17: "No weapon that is formed against you shall prosper, and every tongue that shall arise against you in judgment, you shall show to be in the wrong. This (peace, righteousness, security, triumph over opposition) is the heritage of the servants of the Lord. This is the righteousness or vindication which they obtain from Me—this is that which I impart to them as their justification—says the Lord" (Amplified version). I was so excited that I immediately wrote out the scripture on the back of the director's letter.

Also during prayer I thought of the Christian Law Association, a Christian legal organization that defends churches and Christian schools against local bureaucratic attack. Calling CLA, I explained our situation. Their advice was to stand firm and that they would help us. They sent us a copy of a legal brief which in essence said that a Christian school is a ministry of the church, and if one is zoned for a church, one is automatically zoned for a school.

I took a copy of the brief and the letter to the planning department. Handing them to the director, I drew his attention to the scripture that I had written out. The director was not impressed. Not being a Christian, this scripture meant nothing to him. Yet I sensed more than ever that God would give us the victory in this situation. All we had to do was stand firm in Him.

The legal brief was turned over to the town attorney with whom I met a few days later. He admitted that the brief was legally correct, but he had found a loophole that he would use to try and shut down the school.

Since the town had just been incorporated the previous year, all the churches within the city limits were automatically grandfathered into the zoning system at that time. He argued that since we were grandfathered in and not zoned by the process of application, we needed to apply for a permit for the church, and then everything would be legal. The church, by the way, had been at its present location for over twenty years. We saw this as a clever ruse to get us to submit an application for a permit for the church. We did so nonetheless on the advice of our attorney.

A short time later we received from the town-planning department a document to be signed by the pastor, granting us a permit for the church on condition that we not operate a day school. We consulted with CLA. They advised us not to accept this condition but to return the document unsigned, and continue to operate the school. The CLA also advised us to appeal the decision of the planning commission to the town council, which we did.

At this point, we learned that a neighbor who objected to the school had filed a complaint with the town. This information prompted me to visit all of our neighbors with a petition in favor of the school. Of the twenty or so neighbors, only two did not sign the petition in our favor.

Meanwhile, a member of the town council found out about our favorable petition, which was also signed by most of my local pastor friends. This council member took it upon himself to canvas our neighborhood with the express purpose of persuading our neighbors to change their minds about the school. Some did.

Finally, we had a showdown with the town council at a public meeting. The meeting place was crowded to overflowing, mostly with supporters of the school. Input was requested and given by the various town departmental heads and of these, only one supported the school.

The outcome of the meeting was that our appeal was denied, and a short time later we received a citation for violation of Civil Code No. so and so with a court date to show cause.

This began a two-year litigation process. It seemed that the local judge found himself on the horns of a dilemma. He did not want to rule against the church, but neither did he want to rule against the town. He kept continuing the hearings month after month. Meanwhile, the local media sided with the town, even though we had good support from the community at large. Fair-minded people recognized that we were being unfairly treated.

Finally, the local judge found a way out through a conflict of interest issue. An outside judge was brought in to handle the case. He began to get down to business.

We had opted for a judge rather than a jury decision. The judge heard both sides with testimony from various people, including myself as pastor. As I prayed for wisdom I became mindful of Luke 12:11-12, "And when they bring you before the synagogues and the magistrates and the authorities, do not be anxious (beforehand) how you should reply in defense or what you are to say. For the Holy Spirit will teach you in that very hour and moment what you ought to say" (Amplified).

I told the judge that I was convinced of the necessity for Christian education, and that the school was a ministry of the church. I quoted the scripture, "We must obey God rather than men"(Acts 5:29).

The judge found that we were not in violation. He ruled in favor of the school ministry continuing. The Holy Spirit had faithfully guided us.

In all of this time, we had not received a bill from our local attorney. By now the fees could have been well over one hundred thousand dollars. I called him and asked him to submit a bill.

"Pastor," he responded, "There will be no bill. I felt God telling me to do this as unto Him without charge."

There followed an upsurge of support for the church school in the community. It is interesting to note that every town departmental head lost his job but the one who had supported the church school. God's promise in Isaiah 54:17 was fulfilled.

The school has now been in operation for many years. Yvonne was principal for eleven of those years, often putting in twelve hour days. During that time she was affectionately known as "Mrs. O." She paid a big price for the ministry of Christian Center School, even to the detriment of her health.

Our objective in operating Christian Center School has been to obey the imperatives of God's Word: "You shall love the Lord your God with all your heart and with your entire being and with all your might. And these words, which I am commanding you this day, shall be (first) in your own mind and heart; (then) you shall whet and sharpen them, so as to make them penetrate, and teach and impress them diligently upon the (minds and) hearts of your children" (Deuteronomy 6:5-7, Amplified).

Our school Scripture and motto is taken from 2 Timothy 2:15: "Study and be eager to do your utmost to present yourself to God approved (tested by trial) a workman who has no cause to be ashamed, correctly analyzing and accurately dividing—rightly handling and skillfully teaching—the word of truth" (Amplified).

Teaching is training. Training for life must include training for eternity. The goal of the school is not to reform, but to train Christian youth in the highest principles of Christian leadership, self-discipline, responsibility, integrity, and citizenship. Christian Center School stands without apology for the Gospel and the highest standard of morality and Christian behavior.

Before each school day begins, as the school pastor, I have a time of prayer with each student who arrives during that time. Moving from desk to desk, I pray for each student's spiritual, emotional, physical, and academic needs, as I know their individual backgrounds. Many of the students are being raised by single parents, usually the mother.

I particularly enjoy spending time with the

students out on the playground during recess and at lunch time. This is when they are apt to be the most expressive and open in their conversations. Often the younger children will come up and say, "I want to give you a hug, Pastor." I think they see me as the grandfather they may not have, and find security in the love and discipline I offer them.

The school day opens with assembly. The opening exercises consist of three pledges: one to the Bible, one to the Christian flag, and another to the American flag. Then we recite the memory scripture for the month, which is a minimum of ten verses. By the end of the year they can recite a minimum of one hundred verses!

After a brief praise and worship service, we pray and receive prayer requests from the students. Congratulation slips are distributed for subjects passed the previous day, with special congratulations to those who scored 100% in tests. Then there is a short period of sharing the Word. Once a week we hold chapel for forty-five minutes with the students divided into small groups according to age.

For academics, we use a curriculum from the Accelerated Christian Education School of Tomorrow. Students work at their own academic level in textbook paces. A year's minimum work consists of sixty paces, twelve in each of the five core subjects of math, English, social studies, science and word-building. One foreign language, physical education, Bible, and Computer Literacy round out the requirements. There are electives in music, art, typing, and other subjects.

Merits are gained for the completion of goals, as we emphasize the positive with merits rather than demerits. All students are challenged to make honor roll.

During the first half of the school day, the students concentrate on their academics, and in the afternoon there is opportunity for various electives. Students receive a lot of individual attention. In the learning center, students and staff communicate in a whisper, so as not to disturb other students.

The key to success in this system is the ability to read well. When a student starts in school at five years of age, he or she spends two years learning to read well. Once reading is mastered, students are promoted to the regular Learning Center. We find that students who have mastered reading usually do well in this individualized curriculum.

During the school year, the junior high and high school students prepare for three conventions in winter and spring, and an International Convention in June. In the International Convention, they compete with students from ACE schools around the world—a great learning experience for them.

The original property where the church/school began consisted of one building. Inside was a sanctuary for two hundred people and four small rooms. The building sat on a quarter acre of ground, which left us cramped for space, especially on the playground.

A year after opening the school, our next-door neighbors, an elderly couple, offered to sell us their property at a very reasonable price. This property consisted of a two-bedroom house and a large garage on three-fourths of an acre. Before we could close the sale, the man died suddenly. His widow decided to keep the home for her daughter and two grandchildren.

A short time later, the widow came to me and shared that she felt God was telling her to give us half of her property, which adjoined our school playground.

"I will not be able to sleep until I do this," she

confided.

Naturally, we did not want this poor lady losing any sleep, so we accepted her gift. Thanks be to God, this more than doubled our playground area. She requested a low fence so that she could enjoy seeing the children playing on what now was God's property.

A couple of years later she died and her daughter offered to sell the remaining property to us, provided we would buy her a comparable home. At this point we had some savings and needed to raise $37,000 to secure the new property. The following Sunday I shared with the people that we needed to raise this amount. Our friend Bob, who lived in another area, happened to be present in that service. He was on his way home from an FGBMFI world convention in Rio, where God had moved mightily in his life. Before I began to preach, I asked Bob to come and share his experience.

Bob came to the podium and said, "All I am going to share is what God has just put on my heart. When you mentioned that you needed to raise $37,000, something stirred in my spirit. I had a very strong impression that I was to loan you $37,000 at no interest, to be paid back as you are able."

I almost fell over with excitement. We all thanked God for His awesome goodness to us and for His obedient servant Bob. Within a few days we had the check and were able to close the deal on a replacement house for our neighbor in exchange for her property. With that, we more than doubled our space once more. Praise the Lord!

God's provision has continued faithfully down the years and we have continued to pay our bills on time.

Dark Night of the Soul

At one point in 1992, I came to a place in my ministry which I can only describe as a "dark night of the soul." I felt as though I was walking down a dark tunnel with no glimmer of light at the end. God seemed nowhere around. I could identify with Jesus on the cross when He cried out in agony, "My God, my God, why hast Thou forsaken Me?" It seemed as though God had forsaken me. Yet deep down in my spirit, I knew it was part of God's purifying process in my life—the process of dying to the self, taking up the cross, and following Jesus.

I have often heard that when you reach the end of your rope spiritually, you should make a knot and hang onto God. This is what I was doing—desperately hanging on to God. It was like being out on a limb and the devil sawing it off as he taunted me by saying, "Where is your God now? Why don't you give up and quit the ministry? There has been no fruit. You are a failure."

I was aware, like Moses, that I wasn't going to carry my congregation across the Jordan River. I was tired emotionally, physically, and spiritually of wearing two hats—one for church and the other for school. My heart was with the school, I realized. I felt alive around young people, so that is where my energy went. Consequently, the church was not growing. I knew I was no longer the person to lead them. Gloom pervaded my soul.

One evening a church member called and invited us over to his house to watch a certain program on the Christian Broadcasting Network.

CBN was doing a special program on Hollywood. A group of professional Christian actors were playing a witnessing drama on the street. The program began by interviewing the director of the drama, asking him to share a brief testimony of how he came to be saved.

"About ten years ago," he began, "I had come to the end of my rope. My life had crashed around me and I had gone into total depression. I was in a little coffee shop outside of Fresno with three friends when a guy approached our table and began to speak with a touch of an Irish brogue. He said that God had sent him to rescue someone at our table who was in serious trouble. Obviously, it was me and I blurted out, 'It's me, it's me. I am in serious trouble.' The man explained that he was a pastor in Paradise in northern California, and that he would like to pray for me. As he prayed, the Lord touched me. I accepted Jesus as Lord of my life, along with three of my friends. The pastor left and I have had no contact with him since. I began to read the Bible and to grow spiritually. I've been a Hollywood director, and some years after that incident in Fresno, I began directing Christian drama for witnessing on the streets of Hollywood. That is why we are here today."

As the program ended, I felt tears running down my face. The church member turned to me and grinned, "I knew that pastor had to be you, Vince!"

I nodded, weeping for joy at how God had used my life to touch this Hollywood director. My spirits lifted as I saw how God was using this man mightily to spread the Gospel in a unique way.

As we keep casting our bread upon the water, we

have no idea how many people are being reached with the bread of life, God's Word. It is called the ripple effect. I often think about the one who was God's instrument in leading Billy Graham to the Lord.

I am reminded of a young man that God brought into our fellowship in the early days of the Paradise ministry. Dick was a tall, dark handsome young man with a beautiful wife, Carla, whose blond hair reached down her back in a spectacular fashion. She had been coming to the fellowship for some time. One Sunday evening her husband came with her. I found out later that he only came this one time to please her, as he had just recently been saved in a local non-Pentecostal church.

The teaching that evening was on the baptism in the Holy Spirit. Following the teaching I gave an altar call for anyone desiring to be baptized in the Holy Spirit, and this young man came forward. As we laid our hands on him his prayer language began to sputter out of his mouth like an old John Deere tractor. Pretty soon it was flowing like a river as he was embued with the power of the Holy Spirit.

After this experience, Dick kept coming back for more. His spiritual batteries were all charged up and he was ready to go. We figured that the youth group would be a good outlet for him to exercise his zeal for the Lord. We could see that he had great potential as we observed him minister to the young people, who responded to his enthusiasm and brought their friends.

After about a year, Dick expressed a desire to go to a Bible School out of state. We supported him in his decision and off he went with his wife and three-year-old daughter, having sold all of their worldly possessions to finance this project. Carla also attended classes at the Bible School while pregnant with their second child. It was a very trying time physically and financially, though we helped as much as we could. They persevered through the difficulties of that year. Their baby was due just prior to graduation. I flew out for the ceremony.

Right in the middle of graduation, there was an emergency announcement calling Dick, Carla, and his pastor to a local hospital, where baby Jesse was in critical condition. We rushed to the hospital, all the while praying and interceding on behalf of the baby. Our prayers were answered and their baby boy survived.

A short time later, Dick, Carla, Sarah, and Jesse arrived back in Paradise. Dick picked up with the youth group where he had left off, and again it began to grow.

All this time Dick had a burden for his unsaved extended family members. He and Carla would often go to the San Jose area to witness to them. Soon one got saved, then another and another, until he had five family members to disciple in a Bible study. This fledgling group began to grow and take more and more of his time away from Paradise Christian Center.

Eventually, we released him to move back to San Jose where, in his younger days, he was known as a "hell raiser." Now he is a "hell razer," with many people being born again from above and needing discipling. Soon, a fellowship was formed. We ordained Dick and sent him forth to pastor this new group in San Jose.

At first I was reluctant to let him go, since I recognized his potential and charisma. But God reminded me of Acts 13 where the church at Antioch did not hesitate to send out their very best, Paul and Barnabas.

We prayed daily for our spiritual offspring. As we expected, the San Jose fellowship began to grow and grow, until today Jubilee Christian Center consists of six thousand members and Dick has developed a world-wide ministry.

At the same time, there was another young man, who together with his wife, had been saved at one of the Bible studies prior to our moving to Paradise. They started fellowshipping with us and became close friends of Dick and Carla. Both families went to Bible School together.

Richard and Corrine stayed at the Bible School for a couple of years. By the time he returned to Paradise Christian Center, his friend Dick was already pastoring in San Jose. A year or so later, Richard and his family moved to San Jose to help with the rapidly growing work there. Later, Richard moved to Sacramento where he has been pastoring a church for several years.

Around this same time we had a man in our fellowship who following his salvation, grew rapidly spiritually under the ministry of PCC. He literally devoured the Word of God in systematic daily Bible study and became a very gifted Bible teacher. A group of people who were coming to our fellowship from a neighboring town desired to have their own fellowship. They requested that Tom become their pastor. We laid hands on our gifted Bible teacher and sent him forth to pastor this group. Tom eventually returned to our fellowship to continue his ministry as a Bible teacher. His weekly Bible class grew to a full house. A year later Tom went to be Dean of Faith Bible College, in San Jose, under Dick Bernal's ministry.

After ministering there several years, Tom and his family moved back to Paradise, from where he now has an anointed ministry to pastors in Romania. He spends several months each year teaching the national pastors.

I reminisced over these and other memories as I

struggled to get through my dark night of the soul. I came across an article from the local newspaper concerning a miracle healing that God performed at Paradise Christian Center some years earlier.

One Sunday morning as I was teaching, my attention was drawn to a man who happened to be visiting that day. Faith welled up within me as I found myself addressing him: "Sir, I don't know what your physical condition is, but it seems that you need a healing miracle. God is saying to you that you can reach out to him by faith right now and receive that healing miracle."

He began to weep saying, "Do I ever need a miracle. I have been diagnosed with terminal cancer, but by faith I am going to believe for a miracle from Jesus, the Divine Physician."

He just spoke those words of faith; we did not lay hands on him. I had no more contact with him, but about a year or so later—just when I needed special encouragement from the Lord—I noticed his picture in the local newspaper. The story described how he regularly went to mass, but on a particular Sunday he was led to go to Paradise Christian Center. During the service, he said that God touched him with His healing power and the cancer in his body immediately went into remission.

God showed His loving care on the occasion of our first Minister's Fellowship International annual meeting. Several hundred pastors and elders were chatting away with each other. There I was, sitting in the midst of them—a stranger from Paradise—feeling insecure and wondering to myself and God, *What am I doing here? I don't know these people and they don't even know I exist.*

Pastor Mike Herron began to lead worship with a

powerful anointing. At one point he stopped and said, "I have a word for Vince O'Shaughnessy. Is he here?"

I almost fell off my chair as I heard confirmation that the Lord knew I was there. The word from the Lord had to do with the healing of my heart physically and spiritually. I had been having symptoms of heart trouble. A short time later my doctor gave me all kinds of tests to find out that I had no problem. Praise the Lord for the things He has done.

The Prophecy

In 1992, Yvonne and I both experienced burn-out to the point that we took a sabbatical the following year. When we returned to Paradise Christian Center we began to pray for God to bring about a transition in our lives. In fact, this transition had already begun when Yvonne had stepped down from being principal to office administrator of Christian Center School.

Paradise Christian Center was a member of a large group of churches called Ministers Fellowship International (MFI), with headquarters at Bible Temple in Oregon under the leadership of Pastor Dick Iverson. I wrote to Pastor Iverson and asked him to be on the lookout for a Joshua type of pastor who could come in with fresh energy and lead the fellowship over the Jordan river and into the promised land.

The very next day there was a letter from Pastor Iverson—a letter he had written before receiving mine. His letter to all MFI pastors shared that he was in prayer for a Joshua to come and take over the ministry at Bible Temple. His Joshua soon turned out to be the gifted pastor, Frank Damazio.

In the fall of 1993, at the annual MFI convention, Yvonne and I were ministered to prophetically in a presbytery-type session. I would like to share some excerpts from this prophecy, as it points to where we are today:

You have come to a crossroads. The word of the Lord to you is to stand still and see the salvation of the Lord; stand still for the Lord has His hand upon you. The Lord sees the years of faithfulness, the years of consistency, the years that you have walked in the ways of the Lord and stood fast for the truth of God. The Lord says, in the hours of need, and the hours of decision, "I am not going to forsake you, I am not going to leave you." The word of the Lord to you, brother, is faithfulness and patience right now. Stand still and see the salvation of the Lord.

There are ten thousand instructors in Christ, but there are not many fathers and mothers in the body that people can look to as mentors and as counselors, as people who have a history in God, a background and pattern of life that is unquestionable and above reproach. Yea, the Lord God says to you, that even at this time of change, and a new hour in your life, you are going to continue to stand firm. You are going to be the kind that people will look to.

I see you as mentoring many young ministries. I see you training leaders with the teaching and experience that the Lord God has put within you. The Lord says, "I am going to bring a shift in your ministry, where you are not going to carry on normal ecclesiastical things, but in the days to come you are going to be a trainer of the young men and women who are going to stand in the gap and are going to build up the hedge, and be part of the new generation of ministry I am bringing forth in the earth. Through waiting with patience, and in the timing of the Lord, you will sense, 'I am not being moved out and put on a shelf, but I am being brought to a new place of usefulness.'"

You have felt like you have just been going round and round the mountain. You didn't feel like you were coming to a place where you were seeing something happen. The work of God is not counted by numbers or by those who are before us. The work of God is that which is done in the heart to people that are near and far away. Your lives have touched multitudes throughout the years. The strength of the Lord is going to come upon you so that you can be an imparter of strength, both in the natural and in the spiritual. You will help ministries that are floundering know which way to go. You will speak strength into their lives. God brought you out and brought you into the work of His kingdom.

The Spirit of the Lord is going to take you in and bring you out. I see the hand of the Lord using you not only in the city that you are in, but in other cities, and in other nations. The hand of the Lord has just begun to work in your lives. All that has been stored up in God's spiritual bank in times gone by is going to be released, exploding out of your lives.

I sense very strongly that there is a

real change coming to you in the days ahead, in terms of fulfillment and joy, and contentment in ministry. You are going to be in a capacity of less responsibility in some areas, but more in others. You are going to enjoy the change. You are not marking time as you are being patient and being faithful now—no way! Continue to walk with God, doing what you know to do, and watch God put together His plan and His purpose, where you will be a real father and mother to a lot more people. There will be a new sense of youthfulness coming into you—not a sense of being retired but refired.

Yvonne and I felt overwhelmed with joy and peacefulness in hearing such clear and loving words through the spirit of prophesy.

Amen. Hallelujah! Praise the Lord!

In the fall of 1994, in answer to our fervent prayers, God sent us our Joshua in Pastor Allen Higgins and his wife Beverley. God more than met our request for just the right couple for Paradise Christian Center—a man and a woman of God filled with many spiritual gifts in their ministry. The first part of the prophesy regarding a transition in our ministry was fulfilled.

God's Tomorrow

Yvonne and I continue to minister at Paradise Christian Center School, she as office administrator, and me working in the school. During the past summer we have enjoyed the recess, although there is always work to be done in tying up loose ends from the previous school year, and preparing for the new one.

During the summer we spent time with our precious five-year-old granddaughter, Kaitlyn Maeve, the child of our oldest daughter Kelly. Kelly graduated from business college at the top of her class, then married. She continues to work in the field of accounting while studying to become a CPA.

I recall fondly the occasion of Kelly's water baptism when she was about six years old. It was late on a Sunday afternoon after several adults had left receiving water baptism in our pool. Kelly and I were swimming around in the pool when she said, "Dad, I would like to be baptized also."

We sat on the side of the pool, and I explained in as simple terms as I could the significance of water baptism. I explained to her about the old nature, the old man, passing away and being replaced by new life in Christ (2 Cor 5:17). With that, I went ahead and baptized her by immersion. Kelly immediately sat up on the side of the pool and watched me as I did some laps.

When she didn't jump in and out-swim me as she usually did, I asked, "Kelly, why aren't you swimming?"

Her response shocked and edified me. "Daddy, I don't want to because my old man is dead at the bottom of the pool."

Our youngest daughter, Seana, graduated from college summa cum laude, and has spent the past year with Americorps. She plans on going to graduate school for a masters in world history. When Seana was about four-years-old, we had an evangelist and his wife living with us for about six months. He was very much into deliverance ministry. When people came to our home for this ministry, little Seana often heard him loudly declare, "I rebuke you in the name of Jesus."

One day Yvonne was in the grocery store with Seana tagging along. Suddenly she realized that Seana was not with her. Just then she heard the clatter of stuff falling to the ground. Sure enough, there was Seana in the midst of it all, loudly declaring, "I 'buke' you in the name of Jesus!"

We also have a very precious foster daughter, Jan-Kristine, who has been with us since she was five years old. She attends Christian Center School and is doing quite well.

It has been three years since I wrote my testimony for inclusion in a book entitled, *Far From Rome, Near to God.* This book was published in 1994 and consists of the personal testimonies of fifty former Roman Catholic priests whom God called out of darkness into His marvelous light, and who have continued to minister the light of the Gospel.

I have just written a revised introduction for my testimony, as the book is about to go into the second edition and be translated into foreign languages. The English version has been making its way around the world. I have received many letters and telephone calls which have encouraged me to expand my testimony in the form of this book.

I recently received a letter from New South Wales, Australia.

"I have just read the book with your testimony," wrote the man ". . . and I am wondering if you have your testimony in a tract form that I could distribute in Australia. There are quite a few families of Irish descent who live in this area. Unlike you, I have never been a Roman Catholic, but I have a burden for them and try to reach out to them in love."

I wrote back to this man that my testimony is in tract form and now available.

We are waiting expectantly for the next phase of God's plan for our lives. We are renewing our strength in Him for the days that are ahead, when we will soar again as eagles (Isaiah 40:31).

Right now we are in a holding pattern as to what comes next in life. We had a New Year's Eve get-together at the church. People shared their hopes and dreams for the new year. I found myself saying, "I feel like a plane circling an airport in a thick fog. I'm in a holding pattern and can't see where we're supposed to land."

Associate Pastor Bob McKim jumped up and said, "God just revealed to me that your life is in a holding pattern because God is in the control tower. You're being guided to a God-controlled landing."

I started this book by recalling how a priest and nun came to fall in love, marry, and set out on a journey to serve the Lord their God. As I draw this book to a close, I want to mention that we have grown in our relationship over the years.

I am happy to say that, although it hasn't always been easy, the first love that Yvonne and I found for each other is stronger than ever. This intimacy has matured from the initial emotional bonding to a deep appreciation of each other.

I just `gave Yvonne a 25th wedding anniversary card that sums up a lifetime of feelings for her—my precious wife and soul-mate.

"Dear Yvonne, every time I look at you I simply can't believe you're mine. I love the special qualities I see. I see your sensitivity, your thoughtfulness and humor. And I see the tender love you have for me. Every time I look at you I stop to think how rare it is to have the special kind of love we do. And once again I realize how much I love the life we share, and just how deeply I'm in love with you."

As we look to the future, there is a peace underneath the anxiety we sometimes feel. We don't have all the answers, and we can't control everything that happens. But one thing is as certain as the air we breathe. We are in good hands, because God is in charge, and we live in God's tomorrow.

Our prayer for you is that you may know Jesus more intimately in His resurrection power. If you do not know Jesus in this way, you can pray for a close personal relationship with Him: "Father God, I thank you for Jesus, and for what He has done for me on the cross of Calvary, that I might live eternally. I repent and receive the forgiveness of all the sins of my life. I invite Jesus to come into my heart and be Lord of my life. I invite the Holy Spirit to bless and guide every area of my life. Thank you. In Jesus' name."

Praying this prayer with repentance and sincerity makes you a new creature in Christ, a newborn Christian. To grow in Christ, read the Word of God and find a mature Christian to answer your questions, helping you understand the ways of the Lord. Join a family of believers in a Bible-believing church or fellowship, if you do not regularly attend one. The Gospel of John is an inspiring place to begin your Bible reading.

And here is a word of blessing from an Irish pastor's heart: "Until we meet in heaven, may the Lord keep you and hold you in the palm of His hand."

APPENDIX I:
Baptism of the Holy Spirit

There are two experiences of the Holy Spirit, the first occurring when you are born again. This "born again" experience happened to the disciples when Jesus appeared to them for the first time following His resurrection. Jesus "breathed on them, and said to them, 'Receive the Holy Spirit.'" (John 20:22). No one could be born again until Jesus had been raised from the dead. Why? Because you need to believe in your heart that God raised Jesus from the dead in order to be saved (Romans 10:9).

The disciples' second experience of the Holy Spirit was called the infilling or baptism of the Holy Spirit. That took place fifty days after Christ's resurrection, on the Jewish feast day of Pentecost. "And they were all filled with the Holy Spirit and began to speak with other tongues, as the spirit was giving them utterance" (Acts 2:4).

We find the two types of experiences of the Holy Spirit again in Acts 8, which is the account of Phillip evangelizing Samaria with great success. "And Phillip went down to the city of Samaria and began proclaiming Jesus to them. And the multitudes with one accord were giving attention to what was said by Phillip, as they heard and saw the signs which he was performing. For in the case of many who had unclean spirits, they were coming out of them shouting with a loud voice; and many who had been paralyzed and lame, were healed. And there was much rejoicing in that city. But when they believed Phillip preaching the good news about the kingdom of God and the name of Jesus Christ, they were being baptized, men and women alike" (Acts 8:5-8, 12).

People were believing the good news of salvation and being water-baptized. "When the apostles in Jerusalem heard that Samaria had received the Word of God, they sent them Peter and John, who came down and prayed for them, that they might receive the Holy Spirit. For He had not yet fallen upon any of them; they had simply been baptized in the name of the Lord Jesus. Then they began laying their hands on them and they were receiving the Holy Spirit" (Acts 8:14-17).

These verses describe two distinct experiences involving the Holy Spirit. Peter and John were sent down to Samaria to pray specifically for the new converts to receive the Holy Spirit. They had received the regenerative power of the Holy Spirit—the seal of their salvation—when they were born again, but they had not yet been filled or baptized with the Holy Spirit. They had simply been water-baptized. But when Peter and John laid hands on them, they received the Holy Spirit.

The usual procedure is for people to be water baptized before being baptized in the Holy Spirit, as we have seen in Acts 8. But the opposite takes place in Acts 10, when Peter preaches the gospel in the house of Cornelius: "While Peter was still speaking these words, the Holy Spirit fell upon all those who were listening to the message, and all the circumcised believers who had come with Peter were amazed, because the gift of the Holy Spirit had been poured out upon the Gentiles also. For they were hearing them speaking with tongues and exalting God. Then Peter answered, 'Surely no one can refuse the water for these to be baptized who have received the Holy Spirit just as we did, can he?' And he ordered them to be baptized in the name of Jesus Christ" (Acts 10:44-48).

Again in Acts 19:1-6, the Ephesian believers are baptized with the Holy Spirit and speak in tongues as Paul laid his hands on them: "And when Paul had laid his hands on them, the Holy Spirit came on them and they began speaking with other tongues and prophesying" (Acts 19:6). Notice that they had first been water-baptized in the name of the Lord Jesus.

In Luke 11:1-13, Jesus stresses the importance of persistence in prayer until we are filled or baptized in the Holy Spirit. In Acts 1:8, He tells us that we shall receive power when the Holy Spirit has come upon us, power to be His witnesses "even to the remotest part of the earth."

As born-again Christians, there is only one thing we need to do to receive this power, and that is to ask for it and believe we receive it. "If you then, being evil, know how to give good gifts to your children, how much more shall your heavenly Father give the Holy Spirit to those who ask Him" (Luke 11:13).

Spending time in prayer with Jesus each day empowers us with a holy boldness for witnessing to friends, family, workers, and even strangers about the reality of Christ in the world. It is not a matter of choice whether or not to be His witnesses. We are commanded in the great commission in Matthew 28:19-20: "Go, therefore, and make disciples of all the nations, baptizing them in the name of the Father and of the Son and of the Holy Spirit, teaching them to observe all that I commanded you; and lo, I am with you always, even to the end of the age."

When it comes to witnessing for Jesus, it is very important not only to have holy boldness, but especially to have wisdom and discernment. We must sense when to speak and when to remain silent. Otherwise, our witness can come across to others as self-righteous, brash, or ill-timed, insulting them instead of inspiring them. Jesus tells us in Matthew 7:6: "Do not give what is holy to the dogs, and do not throw your pearls before swine, lest they trample them under their feet, and turn and tear you to pieces." By asking and allowing the Holy Spirit to show us when people are open and ready to receive the gospel message, we increase the sensitivity of our witness.

Yvonne and I have tried various approaches to witnessing. At one stage, we went from door to door with very little response. Later, we recognized that this lack of receptivity in people seemed to be correlated with our lack of fervent prayer prior to calling on them. When we corrected this by spending more preparatory time in pray, we usually had a slightly better response.

Then we got involved in "power evangelism," which means that we relied on the guidance of the Holy Spirit to lead us to the homes of those who were ready to receive the message of the gospel. An example is when two of our men walked down a certain street praying for the Holy Spirit to guide them. Suddenly they felt led to go to a particular house. When they told the man who answered the door that they had come to share the full gospel message, his response was, "I have been praying all day long for God to send someone who would pray with me for the baptism of the Holy Spirit." Praise God, they prayed with him and he received.

The bottom line for success in evangelism, or indeed any area of ministry, is prayer and more prayer. The story is told of Pastor Yonggi Cho who pastors the largest church in the world. He was asked the reason for this tremendous success, and his response was "I pray and I pray and I pray and then I pray some more." He established a place of continuous prayer, twenty-four hours a day, called Prayer Mountain. Here, thousands of Christians take turns praying and interceding before God on a continuous basis.

This approach might seem daunting to some Christians. I would suggest that the key to being a faithful witness is simply asking the Holy Spirit for daily guidance, and then doing what He impresses upon you.

BIBLIOGRAPHY

Bennett, Richard, et al, 1994 *Far From Rome, Near To God,* Associated Publishers, Inc. Lafayette, IN 47803.

McCarthy, James G. 1995 *The Gospel According to Rome,* Harvest House Publishers, Eugene, Oregon.

Montgomery, Dan, *Beauty in the Stone: How God Sculpts You into the Image of Christ*, Thomas Nelson Publishers.

Montgomery, Dan, *God and Your Personality,* Pauline Books & Media.

Information and inquiries can be sent to
Vincent and Yvonne O'Shaughnessy
P.O. Box 625
Paradise, California 95967-0625